erts

"*Kids' Brains & Scre*… so many aspects of digital life, it covers the science …esting, accessible, and useful to young people. The book is ideal for any school that has a digital media course, for any parent who wants to talk with their adolescent about why they have the family policies they do, and for any young person who can see that digital childhood is damaging some of their friends. The book shows ways out of the trap, ways to regain a human childhood that is full of real-world fun."

—**Jonathan Haidt**, Thomas Cooley Professor of Ethical Leadership, New York University—Stern School of Business, author of The New York Times No. 1 bestselling *The Anxious Generation: How the Great Rewiring of Childhood Is Causing an Epidemic of Mental Illness*, co-author of *The Coddling of the American Mind*

"*Kids' Brains & Screens* is a fantastic and valuable contribution to any family. It delivers information families and young people need to know in an engaging, kid-friendly way. I will definitely be recommending this to families I work with."

—**Dr. Anna Lembke**, MD, Stanford University Professor and Medical Director of Addiction Medicine—Yale University, author *Drug Dealer, MD: How Doctors Were Duped, Patients Got Hooked, and Why It's So Hard to Stop* and *The New York Times* bestseller *Dopamine Nation: Finding Balance in the Age of Indulgence*

"One of the most harmful, if not THE most harmful, influences on healthy mental, cognitive, and physical health in kids is screens. Every parent knows this but feels ill-equipped to do anything about it. Finally, we have an answer to this problem that really works! I don't know of any other resources that help parents and kids more effectively when it comes to navigating the frightening world of screens."

—**Dr. Meg Meeker**, MD, international bestselling author of *Strong Fathers, Strong Daughters*

"As parents, we have many resources to learn about how dangerous screens are for our kids. What we need is a book for the kids! This is the book we need. I will recommend it to all my patients."

—**Dr. Leonard Sax**, MD, PhD, family physician and author of the The New York Times bestseller *The Collapse of Parenting, Boys Adrift, and Girls on the Edge*

"We're learning that one of the best ways to prevent unhealthy tech use is by teaching kids about the brain. This book empowers kids and provides a solid foundation that parents can build on for years to come. I highly recommend it!"

—**Dr. Victoria Dunckley**, MD, psychiatrist and author of *Reset Your Child's Brain: A Four-Week Plan to End Meltdowns, Raise Grades, and Boost Social Skills by Reversing the Effects of Electronic Screen-Time*

"This is the book I have been waiting for. It is the answer to how to work with your kids, really."

—**Kim John Payne**, MEd, executive director of Simplicity Parenting, author of *Simplicity Parenting, The Soul of Discipline*, and *Emotionally Resilient Tween and Teens*

"The ScreenStrong Kids' Brains & Screens offers families medical research and practical steps to help our kids avoid phone addiction so we aren't lost in the current of 'but everyone else does it so I guess it won't hurt.' I think this is a wonderful support system that modern parents need."

—**Erin Napier**, host of *Home Town* and founder of Old School Parents Raising Engaged Youth

Praise From Experts

"ScreenStrong has developed an interactive and thought-provoking curriculum so that our kids can understand the impacts of screen use. ScreenStrong's program may be the first line of defense to protect our kids by empowering them to be safe and educated about the impact of these technologies."
—**Dr. Jennifer McCauley**, MD, adjunct assistant professor in pediatrics, diplomate of the American Board of Pediatrics

"For the past decade, I have been looking for a science-backed resource for kids, teens, and their families. With the ScreenStrong *Kids' Brains & Screens* student course, we have exactly what I have been looking for to guide families to healthy relationships with the ever-present screens. My hope is that this book will make it into the hands of every child, teen, and family in the world! I can confidently say that there is no greater resource available."
—**Dr. Adriana Stacey**, MD, board-certified psychiatrist and mother of four

"This remarkable course will appeal to your students and help them understand how to gain control over technology rather than have technology control them. Nothing could be more important for their emotional health and academic success!"
—**Richard Freed**, PhD, psychologist and author of *Wired Child Reclaiming Childhood in a Digital Age* and *Better Than Real Life: How Silicon Valley's Secret Science of Persuasive Design Is Stealing Childhood*

"As a pediatric emergency room physician, I've seen an increased number of kids being admitted for anxiety and depression, and the emerging research is showing just how influential screens are on the mental health of children. This book is a fantastic and fun resource to help kids understand the brain science behind screen usage and why it's important to change their habits now to live in a healthier way."
—**Dr. Cody Carpenter**, MD, pediatrician

"I highly recommend the ScreenStrong course to be included in every school science and/or health course as it details in simple language the biological effects of screens on brain and body development. Every student should have this information to guide them toward healthy and balanced use of screens."
—**Cris Rowan,** OT, author of *Virtual Child* and creator of Reconnect Webinars

"This is one of the most comprehensive yet accessible resources on this complex topic that I've come across. It manages to tackle the science and psychology behind the issues created by tech overuse while making it relatable and true to young people's experiences. It's an amazing resource for children, caregivers, and educators alike."
—**Matt Miles**, coauthor, *Screen Schooled: Two Veteran Teachers Expose How Technology Overuse Is Making Our Kids Dumber*

"This well-designed, easy-to-use workbook is an absolute must for any parent or teacher who wants to raise screen-savvy kids. No issue today is as central to the health and happiness of our children as screen use and abuse. Young people who use this resource will absolutely have the foundation to make smart decisions when it comes to the role of screen use in their lives. This is truly a gift to families everywhere!"
—**Joe Clement,** coauthor, Screen *Schooled: Two Veteran Teachers Expose How Technology Overuse Is Making Our Kids Dumber*

Praise From Parents

"This book is truly life-changing. I knew something was off in how my teens were getting drawn into video games more and more. I knew their hours of gaming were wrong, but I lacked the evidence and tools to really explain it to them. Repeating the phrase, 'it's just not how I grew up,' is not as convincing as the research and data found in this book. This book helped my entire family understand the rightful place of screens in our lives. Our family is stronger, more honest with each other, and more connected to others with the help of ScreenStrong. We're surrounded by a storm of culture that pushes technology on our kids at younger and younger ages. ScreenStrong is the lighthouse."
—Josh, father of six

"Once kids and their parents read this engaging resource, they'll fully grasp how smartphones, social media, and video games are designed to keep them hooked—pulling them away from real-life experiences and relationships. This science-backed book empowers families to break free and embrace a healthier, more connected life. How I wish we'd had *Kids' Brains & Screens* when our adult children were younger."
—Amy, mother of four

"My 14-year-old can not put this book down. I found him curled up on the sofa reading it the day we got it in the mail. (It has been a long time since he has read a real book!) He took it in the car on errands yesterday, and yesterday, I was looking for it to show a friend, and it was in my son's room on his nightstand! He never reads at night! Thank you, ScreenStrong, for this incredible resource for my family. It is already changing our lives. We finally have common ground to discuss screen limits together with no fighting. There is something about this book that works. Thank you, ScreenStrong! I think you have just saved my tween from some really big screen mistakes."
—Amanda, mother of three

"This is a resource that parents and grandparents have needed for a long time. It explains the science so well to middle schoolers who need to hear it. The art is amazing which brings the content to life. Parents will save a lot of money on counselors if they get this book for their kids and read it with them."
—Pam, grandmother

"Thank you for being bold and willing to educate us on the fact that we weren't protecting our kids from harm when it came to screens! Because of the *Kids' Brains & Screens* book, my wife and I found the strength and encouragement needed to wean all 4 of our children completely off screen time over about 6 weeks! After reality hit us in the face (everything brought to light in the book) we had no other choice. We felt like we lost our 12-year-old due to his dopamine imbalance, but we got him back to loving regular life activities and accomplishments! What you do is helpful and needed so badly in this time. With the highest gratitude possible, thank you for helping us overcome this challenge!"
—Brian, father of four

"Going through the student course with my 12-year-old son allowed me to share with him the real truth behind what's happening to his developing brain when he's on a screen. We had so many great conversations about difficult topics in a nonconfrontational way, which were edifying to who he is and what he needs to grow into a strong, smart, confident young man. For weeks afterward, he kept asking me questions and wanting to learn more. I feel so capable of raising him in this culture with all the calm and clarity the student course has provided for our family."
—Emily, mother of two boys

Praise From Kids

"As a teen who developed a screen addiction at an early age, education on brain development, how screen addiction evolves, and how to reverse childhood screen addiction were vital to me successfully rewiring my brain. *Kids' Brains & Screens* provides the weapons kids and teens need to fight for their minds. This book equips my generation with the knowledge on how to rewire our brains and teaches us how to use technology as a tool and not let technology use us as its tool instead. As a teen whose mind was taken captive by screens, I can attest that *Kid's Brains & Screens* is one of the tools that will set your mind free from the slavery of screens!"
—Halie, age 19

"This book is awesome! I never knew screens could mess with my brain, but now I get why my parents say no sometimes. It taught me how to keep my brain strong and not get stuck on screens all the time. I'm even sleeping better and having more fun with my friends!"
—Jake, age 10

"I used to feel like I had to be on my phone all the time, but this book showed me how screens really affect my brain and mood. Now, I'm spending way less time online and having more fun doing things I love. I feel happier and way less stressed!"
—Emily, age 12

"This book helped me understand why too much screen time isn't good for my brain. Now I like playing outside more, and I feel really good! It taught me how to be strong and not need my tablet all the time."
—Mia, age 7

"I always thought I needed to be online to stay connected with friends, but this book opened my eyes. It showed me how screens mess with my focus and my mood. Now I'm choosing to spend less time on my phone and more time doing things that make me feel good, like sports and hanging out in real life."
—Alex, age 14

"I absolutely loved this book! It's packed with insightful scientific information and dives deep into important topics that are often overlooked. After reading it, I've been able to help my friends understand the serious dangers of excessive screen time. This book is an eye-opener and an essential read for anyone looking to make informed decisions about their digital habits!"
—Isaac, age 16

"Being part of a ScreenStrong family has truly changed my life. This book helped me understand the real impact screens can have on my brain, and it has been a game-changer for my mental health. Since learning from it, I've become more mindful of my screen time, and I've seen a dramatic improvement. I would 100% recommend this book to anyone looking to improve their well-being by reducing screen time. It's a must-read for anyone serious about reclaiming mental clarity in a world that's constantly plugged in!"
—Olivia, age 18

KIDS' BRAINS & SCREENS

"Kids' Brains and Screens is an extraordinary book!"
—Jonathan Haidt, Author of The Anxious Generation

KIDS' BRAINS & SCREENS

Empowering Kids to Overcome Screen Addiction

HOME EDITION

MELANIE HEMPE, BSN

Artwork & Cover Design: Drobnick Designs LLC

First edition 2025

ISBN: 979-8-9919652-0-0
Printed in the United States of America.

Purchase Code: KBSHOME1226

Other books by Melanie Hempe
The ScreenStrong Solution
Will Your Gamer Survive College
Can Your Teen Survive—And Thrive—Without a Smartphone

Disclaimer: The information in this book does not replace the medical therapy that may be necessary to help an at-risk child or teen. The information provided here is not intended to substitute for medical advice. Instead, all information, content, and materials are for general informational purposes only. Because each individual is unique, please consult your healthcare professional for any medical questions.

For Adam—your story has been a lifeline for countless families. Because of you, ScreenStrong exists, and because of your journey, many young lives and families have been spared the pain of screen addiction. Thank you for turning your challenges into hope for others.

Table of Contents

Welcome to ScreenStrong

We're so glad you found us!

If you're reading this, chances are your family has felt the impact of screens—meltdowns when unplugging, conflicts over screen limits, lost interest in real-life hobbies and family activities, and strained social relationships. You're not alone, and more importantly, there's hope.

This book is filled with powerful stories and proven solutions to help your family break free from screen struggles and reclaim the connection, peace, and joy you may be missing.

And this is just the beginning. When you're done, scan the QR code to unlock a wealth of free resources—educational tools, expert guidance, and a supportive community of families on the same journey. You don't have to navigate this alone.

Connect. Learn. Grow. *Your family's fresh start begins now, and we're here to support you every step of the way!*

Additional ScreenStrong Resources Include:

- *Free Connect Forum for parents*
- *Connect Plus Forum & 30-Day Digital Reset*
- *KBS Parent Edition*
- *ScreenStrong Families Podcast*
- *Phone-Free School Resources Guide & School Posters*

Scan the QR code or visit ScreenStrong.org to unlock these valuable resources and MORE!

INTRODUCTION

Melanie Hempe

Do you ever find yourself worrying about your kids' screen time? If you're like most parents, it's a constant concern—*How much is too much? Are video games harming my kids? Is social media really that bad? When is the right time to give them a smartphone?*

These questions led to countless conflicts in our home, especially with our oldest son, Adam, who played video games almost constantly. I didn't enjoy my role as the "Game Cop Mom," setting timers and enforcing screen limits. We lived in frustration and confusion for years until, finally, Adam's video games became more important than his studies, and he dropped out of college. That was our wake-up call.

Around that same time, I considered giving our middle school daughter, Melissa, a smartphone as she entered high school. I asked my high school parent friends for advice, and their responses were sobering. Many shared that giving their daughters smartphones with social media access was their biggest parenting regret. They confided that their daughters were struggling with anxiety, with most on medication, and even recommended that I contact the physician they all used. Some even suggested I start Melissa on medication preemptively. That was all I needed to hear. Our daughter thrived with a basic phone, free from social media, throughout high school.

After watching our family—and so many others—struggle with the unintended consequences of our screen experiments, I knew I had to find answers. As a nurse, I dove deep into the research, uncovering the biology and science behind screen addiction. It didn't take long to realize that my son was right when he said, "That game did something to me." These screens weren't just harmless entertainment; they were triggering the same brain chemicals as addictive drugs and physically reshaping his developing mind.

Armed with this knowledge, we made a bold decision for our younger children: we removed access to the most addictive and harmful screens—video games, smartphones/social media, and pornography. We had plenty of fun family movie nights and they used their laptops for school, but our entertainment hours were spent offline. In time, we discovered that what seemed radical at first was actually a simple, common-sense solution to a complex problem. This decision transformed our home—and it can transform yours, too.

The **first step** is understanding the science behind screen overuse and its impact on adolescent brain development. This knowledge helps you step back from societal pressures and recognize the warning signs of screen dependency:

- Increased time spent on screens.
- Meltdowns when asked to unplug.
- Conflicts over limits and rules.
- Loss of interest in previously enjoyed activities.
- Strained relationships with family and peers.

The **second step** in transforming your home and your family's relationships with screens is to replace common myths and blindspots with facts:

- Kids don't "binge and go crazy later" when limits are set, especially in a connected family environment.
- They won't be "friendless" without video games or social media—in fact, they often develop deeper, more meaningful in-person friendships.
- "Balance and moderation" is not always the answer; we don't balance things that are inherently harmful—like addictive activities and substances.
- Teaching social media "under your roof" doesn't prepare children to use it responsibly any more than practicing drinking would prevent alcohol abuse.
- Believing your teen is "more mature than most" can be a trap—intelligence is not the same as emotional maturity.

With logic, science, and clear boundaries, you can win the screen battle.

This book provides the **foundational education** you and your children need to understand why avoiding addictive screens—video games, social media/smartphones, and pornography—through adolescence is both healthy and easier than you can imagine.

Consider the story of one of the most significant medical discoveries of all time: handwashing. This simple solution was initially dismissed because it seemed too basic for such a complex problem. Yet today, handwashing is our first line of defense against germs. Similarly, addressing screen overuse may feel radical at first, but eliminating toxic screens can profoundly impact your child's future.

For Parents. This book will give you the confidence to move forward and reclaim your kids from the digital world. You will learn that the benefits of toxic screen use will never outweigh the risks. This book will help you resolve the conflicts, retire you from the role of "Screen Cop," and, contrary to myths, deepen your relationship with your kids instead of weakening them. Imagine a home where screen time isn't a source of constant arguments, instead, your family enjoys connection, laughter, and real life together.

For Teens. This book is for you, too. Be inspired to reclaim your time and reach your highest potential. You can thrive without the constant pull of your devices and make choices that lead to less stress and anxiety. I hope you'll rediscover the fun found in the real world. I hope you will engage with your family more, so you will not regret the lost hours in the virtual world—which, for most kids, is about

16,000 hours of lost time! Embrace this time to invest in your life story, grow deep friendships, discover your gifts and interests, and create memories you won't regret.

Let's dive into the science, embrace simplicity and logic, and create a life where everyone thrives—free from the grip of toxic screens. This journey isn't just about cutting screen time; it's about strengthening families, unlocking potential, and rediscovering the joy of real-life connections.

Despite the years of struggle, I often find myself grateful for Adam's story. His experience not only saved his younger siblings from screen addiction, but also shaped our mission. I hope his story helps save your family, too.

Welcome to ScreenStrong!

Melanie

A NOTE FROM SKIPPY THE CAT

Hey there, cool cats! I'm Skippy, your purr-fect guide throughout this book. You'll spot me at the top of each chapter and in the illustrations (I'm a big deal around here). I'm here to help you "pounce" on all the important info and "purr-sist" through this adventure. Let's have a paws-itively great time learning about screens together! Ready? Let's get started!

ADAM'S STORY

A former gamer

When I was little, I would go to my neighbors' houses, knock on the doors, and ask the parents if my friends could play. We would head out to the woods behind our house or to the vacant lot in our neighborhood to play pick-up baseball or some games we invented. This was my extracurricular activity before video games became popular.

In middle school, we began to play some very fun, innocent video games. My parents set limits, but my interest was already sparked. My gaming life took off when I received my own personal school laptop in ninth grade. By the time I left high school, I had logged over 6,000 hours on video games. I was so dedicated that I didn't have much of a social life in high school.

Going to college freed up even more time for gaming. It was the most important thing in my life. It became my reality. Gaming was the main source of my sense of purpose and self-worth. At this point in my freshman year, I entered the euphoric gaming trance, which most people refer to as "depression." I was so committed to gaming that I didn't even leave my room for classes one week, but my gaming performance was top-notch. After that semester, I was in no shape to continue my college career, so I returned home and joined the Army.

A gamer always thinks about gaming; his world is the virtual world, and the real world is just a nuisance that pulls him away from his reality. Everything he does in the real world is done in order to get back to the gaming world as quickly as possible. His natural state is finding comfort in playing video games. When the gamer progresses in the game, his subconscious mind believes that he is progressing in real life. But he is not.

You can't make meaningful progress with anything in the real world in 10 minutes like you can in a video game. Most accomplishments in life take lots of time, energy, practice, and grit. This causes the gamer to lose interest in real-world activities because nothing can measure up to the pace of video games. His brain has literally been wired to think that his success and productivity lie with video games and that everything else is a waste of time because it isn't as efficient.

"You will never be able to achieve anything truly great if you spend all of your time playing video games."

I wish I had all my gaming hours back. I often imagine what my life would be like if I had spent my time differently, doing something productive. I enjoyed piano when I was young but quit in middle school. I dabbled in tennis in high school but was more compelled to develop my virtual game than my tennis game.

Today, I have filled my gaming void with other productive things: completing college and law school, reading, meeting new people, building relationships, and pursuing a career in law. I finally feel productive with purpose in the truest sense.

Today, many kids sit inside and waste their childhood playing video games. Kids don't even get a childhood anymore. Video games have advanced so quickly and are so prevalent that kids in elementary school are as deep into their gaming "careers" as I was in college, and they haven't even hit double digits yet.

A few words to my fellow gamers.

If you are a gamer, I wish I could talk to you in person and tell you it isn't worth it. You only have one time in your life to be a kid. You may not understand the long-term effects, so you need to learn the science behind gaming and make the logical decision, not an emotional one, to get off your game. Do not be mad at your parents if they tell you to get off your games; they can see further in the future than you can. You may not realize it now, but video games will hinder your decision-making abilities to try new hobbies. Games are designed to keep you hooked. That is why it is best to take the ScreenStrong suggestion and eliminate the games for now.

There is no universal law that says you have to be the same person you were yesterday. You can continue down your path and live a life full of mediocrity and regret, or you can decide to pursue the dreams you have pushed aside to make room for gaming. You have the power to make something of yourself and change the world around you, but you will never be able to achieve anything truly great if you spend all of your time on video games.

Adam
Former gamer

Read more of Adam's story in the book *Will Your Gamer Survive College?* by Melanie Hempe

LYDIA'S STORY

A needed change

Seventh grade marked a change in my outlook on life and the start of my mental health journey. It's the year I got social media.

Growing up, I was a happy-go-lucky kid; I was extroverted and loved to talk and share my opinions. As I began spending more time on social media, I slowly started to lose myself. This sounds dramatic, but it's the only way to describe it adequately.

My parents did everything "right" when giving me a phone. They set limits—no phone in bedrooms or bathrooms, no phone during or after dinner—they didn't even allow the phone to have a data plan, just a Wi-Fi connection. But that wasn't enough to limit the effects on my brain. I was coping with our family's move across the country from Iowa to Texas during middle school. I missed my friends back home and spent a lot of time comparing my life to theirs. My mom let me get Instagram to help me stay connected, but in reality, it just programmed me to have FOMO (fear of missing out).

At the end of eighth grade, I got a "real" phone for my birthday—one with data! That year, my parents took me to the beach for my birthday, but I chose to sit under the umbrella checking Instagram because I could finally access it without Wi-Fi. This is when the phone started to become a bigger problem. At the beginning of ninth grade, I got accepted into an art school for creative writing, so I spent upwards of two hours a day on my phone while riding the bus. After I finished my in-class work at school, my classmates and I were on our phones until the bell rang. Once home, I quickly did my homework and wasted several more hours scrolling.

I withdrew from my family and started to experience anxiety and depression. I have vivid memories of leaving my classes thinking I was sick, but it was an anxiety attack. These attacks started whenever I was in a car or would leave my house. At the end of the first semester, I dropped out of art school due to being mentally overstressed. I went to an online public school for the remainder of high school. My mom saw how I was changing, and she didn't know what was causing it—until she connected the dots.

Around this time, my mom met Melanie Hempe, founder of ScreenStrong, and was educated on why I had changed so negatively in three years. It was the constant influence of social media telling me who I was and what I should be struggling with (i.e., anxiety and depression). Because social platforms increase awareness of mental health—which can be good—having mental health issues often becomes glorified and glamorized. I remember the videos and posts that popped up on my feed telling me "why you're depressed" or "five signs you experience anxiety." Social media introduced many mental health problems that convinced me that I had a particular illness even though I did not. My identity was being built as I let Instagram diagnose me. I believed it. I turned from being a social butterfly to an anxious hermit who lost interest in the real world.

Once my mom realized the problem, she promptly took my smartphone away. Our family chose to do the ScreenStrong Challenge right as the pandemic hit. The first couple of weeks were terrible. My anxiety got so bad that I couldn't even sit out on my front porch without freaking out. But I was detoxing from having constant dopamine rushes and unhealthy amounts of stimulation. It was not easy—but it was so worth it! About week three, I started feeling like myself again. I felt like I could breathe easier and started new hobbies like painting and reading. I began to enjoy my life again.

"I learned that human connection is the number one thing that keeps us going. And if a screen replaces that, how can we change the world for the better?"

At the end of 2020, my family moved back to Iowa. Within the first few months, I saw how social media had affected my old friend group. It was sad. I realized that kids of my generation were losing their people skills and empathy for one another. So, one night, I had my defining moment and decided to be free from the screen trap. Since then, I have traveled with my mom, speaking to students about how to avoid the risks screens bring and the importance of mental health issues. I am so happy to be your guide through this course. I believe that education like this gives us the power to inspire change in our generation and generations to come.

My ScreenStrong story was not easy at first, but it became the best thing my parents ever did for me. I learned that human connection is the number one thing that keeps us going. And if a screen replaces that, how can we change the world for the better?

Lydia
ScreenStrong Student

WHAT IS SCREENSTRONG?

ScreenStrong is a nonprofit dedicated to helping families prevent and reverse childhood screen addiction through science-based education. We empower parents and kids of all ages with the knowledge they need to delay smartphones, skip social media, replace video games, and avoid pornography.

Our bold solutions help you break free from addictive technology and ensure healthy screen use at every age.

The result? Strong kids. Strong families.

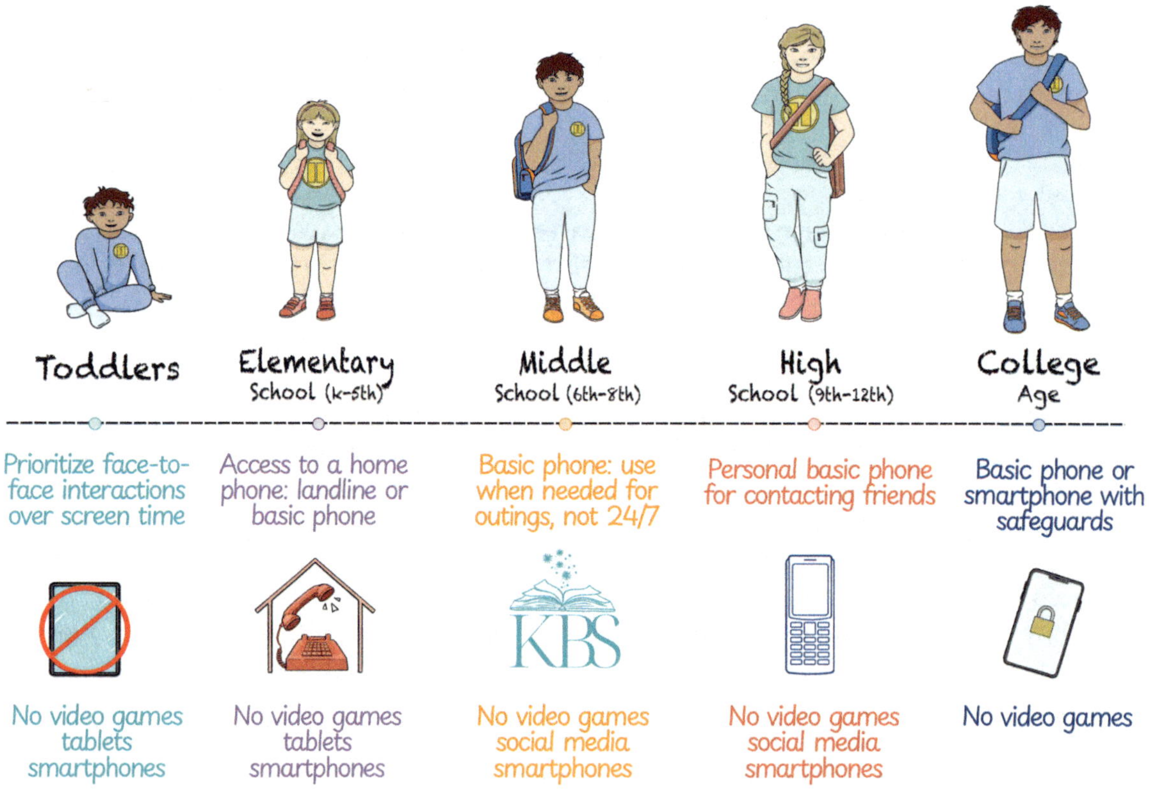

*A "basic phone" is a non-data phone that only allows talking and texting. It does not have internet and does not allow social media apps. If your high schooler wants or needs access to social media, they can use it with your permission through a family account on your phone or laptop.

**See ScreenStrong.org/Resources for basic phone and device safeguard recommendations.

SCREENSTRONG CORE VALUES

BUILD STRONG, HEALTHY FAMILIES

A healthy family thrives when parental influence and leadership outweigh that of peers and screen culture. Strong family bonds at home lay the foundation for lifelong values and resilience.

PROTECT KIDS AND TEENS FROM HARMFUL SCREENS

Technology is a valuable tool, but toxic screen use—social media, video games, pornography—is harmful and not essential for any child or teen. Even in moderation, these high-risk screens can negatively impact brain development and overall well-being.

PRIORITIZE AUTHENTIC RELATIONSHIPS

True human connection grows best through face-to-face interactions, not screen-based communications. Strong friendships and deep relationships are built through shared experiences in the real world.

FOCUS ON REAL-WORLD SKILLS

Life skills matter more than screen skills. Kids and teens thrive when they build independence, confidence, and hands-on abilities that prepare them for success in the real world—not just the digital one.

DARE TO BE DIFFERENT

Saying no to addictive, toxic screens during childhood and adolescence is the best prevention for screen dependency. Being bold is leadership—choosing a ScreenStrong lifestyle means standing out, staying strong, and setting kids up for a healthier, more fulfilling future.

Move your entertainment from the online world back to the real world.
We've Got Your Back!

CHAPTER ONE

YOUR AMAZING BRAIN

CHAPTER 1: INTRODUCTION
YOUR AMAZING BRAIN

Welcome to Chapter One.

The brain is an amazing tool and a complex organ that takes years to develop fully. Thanks to advanced technology, scientists now understand how the brain grows and functions differently in children and teens than in adults.

Here's something cool: your brain develops from the back to the front. The back, which controls movement and balance, develops first, while the front—where big decisions, reasoning, and self-control happen—is the last to mature fully, but not until your mid-twenties.

In this chapter, you'll learn how screen use impacts brain structure and why balancing screen time with real-life activities can help make your brain stronger. You'll be glad you know this now—it'll help you stay ahead of any challenges screens might throw your way!

As you read, keep an eye out for answers to these key questions:

1. *What are the cells that connect different areas of the brain?*
2. *At what age will your brain finish developing?*
3. *What activities can you do to make your brain stronger?*

Let's get started—your brain is about to get a whole lot stronger!

Adam

SECTION 1
HOW DOES MY BRAIN WORK?

> "Albert Einstein's brain was 15% bigger than the average male brain. That's a lot of white matter! No KITTEN!"
>
> *Skippy, The ScreenStrong Cat*

OUR BRAINS ARE THE CONTROL CENTER OF OUR BODIES

The brain is the most important organ in the human body.

This small organ directs and coordinates our movement, actions, and reactions. While it may be only 2% of our body weight, it takes 20% of our energy.

The brain contains approximately 86 billion **neurons,** which relay messages through the spine and across the body. If it were a computer, it could hold up to three million hours of video recordings!

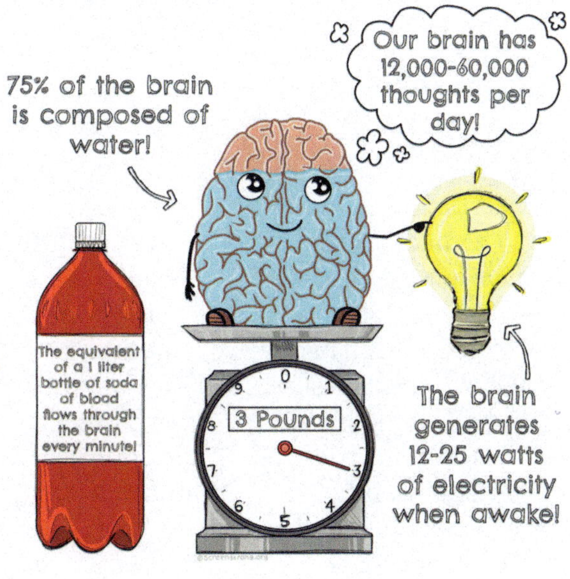

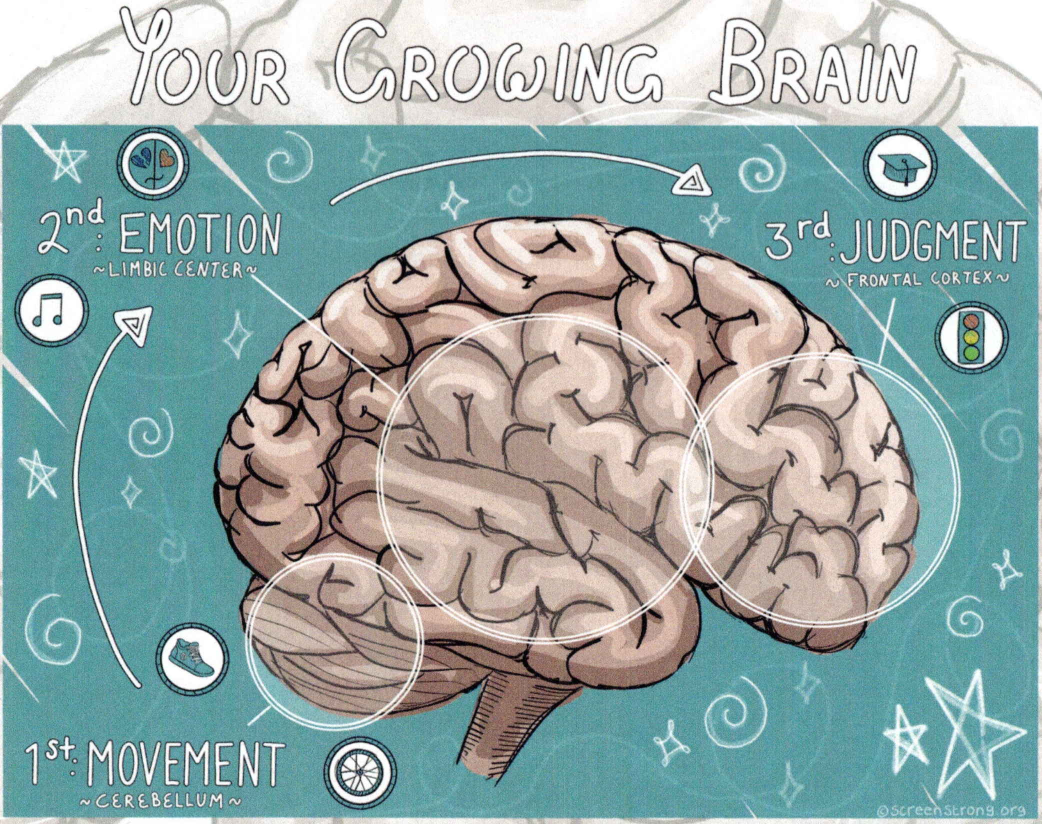

1st

THE **MOVEMENT** CENTER

cerebellum

The **back of the brain** is the first to complete development. This is where simple tasks like movement and balance are processed. It holds more than 50% of the brain's neurons.

2nd

THE **EMOTION** CENTER

limbic center

The **middle of the brain** is the reward center. This is where emotion, memory, and motivation are experienced. This is also the area that is the most active when we are playing on interactive screens.

3rd

THE **JUDGMENT** CENTER

frontal cortex

The **front of the brain** helps us make good decisions, plan ahead, and control impulses. The frontal cortex won't be fully connected and developed until around our 25th birthday.

THE ACCELERATOR WORKS BEFORE THE BRAKES!

Our brains started developing even before we were born. During our younger years, our brains grew rapidly, but in a very specific order, back to front. Think of the brain like a race car. The **back and middle parts of the brain are like the accelerator**—responsible for movement, emotions, rewards, and taking risks. They develop first. The **front of the brain is like the brakes**—responsible for good judgment, impulse control, and wisdom. It develops last. Unfortunately, the accelerator works before the brakes are fully developed. As teenagers, we're in a developmental phase where we tend to take more risks. However, our judgment center isn't fully connected yet to guide us effectively. Yikes!

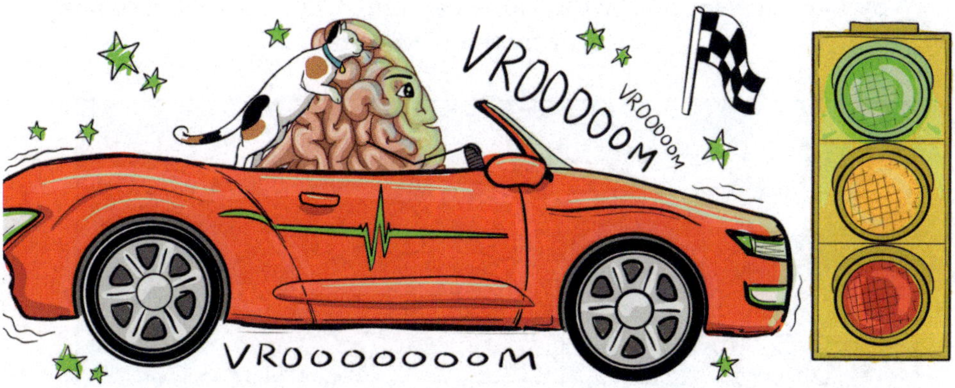

Isn't it good to finally know why we can be emotional and take risks one minute and then be calm and rational the next? This is due to the order of brain development. There is nothing wrong with us. **We need to be patient while our brain development catches up.** We are always learning and becoming more intelligent, but growing up and becoming mature isn't something we can force or speed up.

HOW DOES THE BRAIN WORK? NEURONS.

Every new activity we encounter from birth excites us and causes our neurons to form connections. The brain doesn't just get physically larger; it **grows by strengthening pathways between neurons.** For example, neural pathways strengthen when we talk and move, causing us to develop language and coordination skills. As the brain becomes more complex, it becomes more efficient, and its structure changes.

Let's learn more about the communication network in our brains.

THE COMMUNICATION NETWORK IN THE BRAIN

Brain tissue contains cells called **neurons, the primary functional cells of the brain**. All the work in our brains is done by these special cells, which look like little trees connected to one another by their branches.

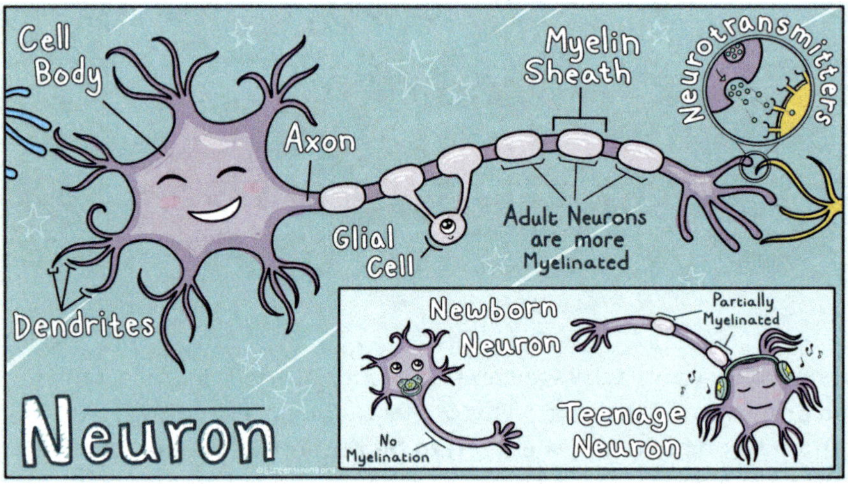

The brain is made up of soft tissue called gray matter and white matter. **The gray matter includes the cell bodies**, where movement, memory, and emotions are controlled. It is located on the brain's outer layer. The **white matter is the myelin** —a white sheath protective coating on the nerves in our brains—that provides structural support and improves the transmission of electrical impulses. It speeds up nerve signals and connects the neurons within the gray matter to each other.

Gray matter contains **nerve cell bodies and dendrites**; white matter contains **axons and myelin**. **Axons** are the extensions of neurons that carry signals to distant parts of the body. Axons can be very long—a single neuron can reach all the way down to your toe! The **glial cells** act to support, protect, and nourish the neuron.

HOW NEURONS TALK TO EACH OTHER

A neural pathway is like a team of connected messengers in our brains.

Neurons chat with different parts of the body, using electrical and chemical signals called **neurotransmitters**.

Think of these pathways as **highways in our brains**, crucial for survival. And guess what? We're always making new pathways. It's like our brains' way of getting stronger and growing smarter. In the first three years of life, 700-1,000 new neural connections form every second!

HOW NEURONS SEND MESSAGES

Neurotransmitters send messages from one neuron (nerve cell) to another at a **speed of up to 260 mph.** Our bodies can't work properly without these special chemicals, sometimes called hormones.

There are many different types of neurotransmitters. One type, acetylcholine, **tells our muscles what to do.** Another kind of neurotransmitter, adrenaline, **makes us feel supercharged when we need extra energy** for something exciting or scary.

A POPULAR NEUROTRANSMITTER

Have you heard of dopamine? It affects our behavior. It is also called the "happy chemical" because it creates pleasure and satisfaction and motivates us to keep doing the things that give us pleasure. We're naturally wired to seek things that make our brains release dopamine. Substances like junk food and activities like gaming and scrolling social media produce a lot of dopamine. These things are so fun that saying no to them is hard.

Did you know that when people take certain stimulant drugs, like cocaine, the brain reacts by releasing too much dopamine? Spending too much time on screens can produce the same high dopamine effects.

HOW TO BUILD A BRAIN

Before we understood brain development, it was believed that teenagers had a fully developed brain, at least from a biological and neurological standpoint.

But now we understand that the brain maturation process, while quite significant during the teenage years, doesn't complete itself until age 25. Let's look at how the brain gets stronger and smarter.

Neuroplasticity

Our brains have the ability to grow new networks quickly **as we learn new skills**. Scientists say our brain is neuroplastic, a strange word meaning that our brains can grow and change through adulthood. Plastic refers to the ability to sculpt, mold, or modify. Our brains are not really made of plastic! However, the majority of brain growth happens during our preteen and teen years.

BUILDING HIGHWAYS IN YOUR GROWING BRAIN

Dirt roads become superhighways.

Think of neural pathways like roads in your brain connecting one place to another. Now think of the **electrochemical signals** as the cars on that road.

When neural pathways are first formed, they start off bumpy, like dirt roads, and signals travel slowly. But, as we use them more, they become smooth, enabling the electrochemical signals to travel much faster. The **neural pathways** we use the most become the fastest highways in the brain. When we actively build these pathways, our brains grow.

Activities build superhighways.

Over time, the activities we do determine how strong our brains become. Activities like playing a musical instrument or running help develop many areas of our brains, paving our neural pathways and making them **permanent.**

The goal is to participate in many activities to form many different brain pathways. Without a variety of neural pathways, we won't be able to perform a wide range of skills. Therefore, we must be thoughtful about our current activities and habits because we are laying the foundation for our future adult brains.

NEURAL PRUNING: THE EFFICIENT BRAIN

Think of neurons as trees in our brains. The dendrites are the branches, the axon is the trunk, and the axon terminals are the roots.

When we're young, the more connections we make with the world, the denser the dendrites on our neurons become, leading to significant brain growth.

There can be thousands of dendrites on each neuron. However, it doesn't stay that way.

Use it or lose it!

Around age 10, to become more efficient, the brain starts **trimming away the pathways that aren't being used**. This process, called **neural pruning,** is like nature saying, "You better use the connections you need, or you'll lose them!"

Our brains clear out unused neural pathways to boost efficiency, making travel on the most frequently used highways easier. It's as if our brains are saying, "Hey, if we're not using these dirt roads, let's shut them down so we can channel our energy into strengthening the roads we ARE using!"

That's why doctors and researchers stress that **the parts of our brains we don't use will shrink while the parts we use get stronger**. This fact underscores the importance of making the most of the teen years. Focus on developing skills, spending time in nature, socializing, and avoiding excessive time spent on mindless screen activities.

LOPSIDED BRAINS

Our brains are not healthy when we pave only a few highways more than all the others.

Screen use often activates or paves the reward pathways in the limbic center rather than strengthening the pathways in the judgment center (frontal cortex). This causes the brain to experience uneven development.

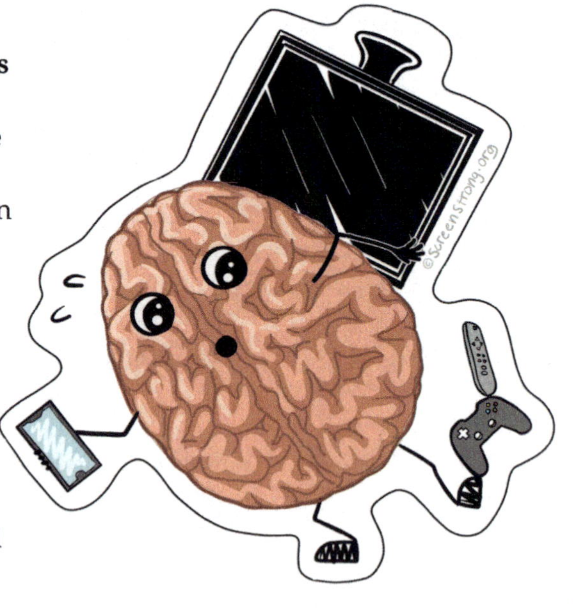

If we spend too much time on screens, our screen habits will become deeply ingrained in our brains, and **our motivation for engaging in healthy habits will decrease.** When we focus on non-screen habits, we are more balanced and will have a healthier brain.

ALL HABITS BECOME PERMANENT

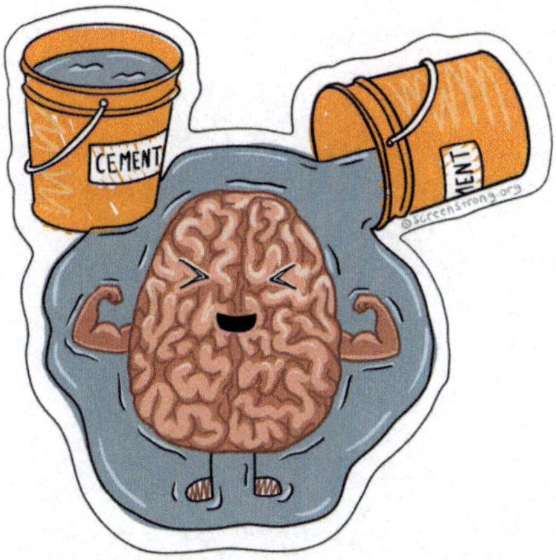

Our brains are designed to make learning habits easier with practice. Fortunately, this makes **good habits** easier (like tying our shoes and riding a bike). Unfortunately, our brains can learn **bad habits** just as easily (like biting our nails or picking up a screen to fill downtime all the time).

Habits are activities that become permanent. In other words, the more time we spend on an activity—good or bad—the **better we get at it and the harder it is for us to undo it or stop.**

Once these habits are formed and the highways are paved in our brains, **they eventually harden like cement**. Many habits are set by our 25th birthday, so creating good habits now will pay off in the future.

UNLOCK YOUR TALENTS NOW WHILE IT'S EASIER!

We possess a valuable gift: the potential to construct many different highways in our brains. Learning skills like a foreign language, a new sport, or a musical instrument is easier while we are young because our neurons are primed for learning. Developing these superhighways now will make us more intelligent and enhance our physical strength and coordination.

Our neurons are eager for us to use them and turn them into superhighways. It's as if they're all saying, "Use me! Use me!" Now is the best time to discover your talents, learn new things, and unlock your potential.

SECTION 2
HOW CAN I IMPROVE MY BRAIN?

"Exercise and sunshine are proven to boost our mood and leave us FELINE good!"

Skippy, The ScreenStrong Cat

Being ScreenStrong enables us to build better brains by focusing on activities that develop strong, diverse brain pathways. Everything we do at this life stage changes and shapes our brains. This is why doctors call the teen years a sensitive period of development—our brains are sensitive to good and bad things. This also explains why it is best to structure our activities to give us the most advantages.

FALL IN LOVE WITH BOREDOM

Interestingly, being bored is one of the **best things for our brains.** Studies reveal that our brains become like an empty canvas ready for creative, innovative ideas when bored. However, many people fear boredom, so they fill all their free time with screen clutter instead, stunting creativity.

Spending time on screens is not downtime like we think. Instead, it robs teen brains of the beneficial effects of boredom. Let's explore more brain-boosting activities on the next page.

BRAIN-BUILDING ACTIVITIES

EXERCISING
When you exercise a lot, your body sends more oxygen to your brain, making it healthier.

CONNECTING WITH FAMILY
When caring adults are a part of your life, you will have better self-esteem, feel less rejected by peers, and experience less sadness and worry. Having fun with your family is one of the best things you can do for brain health.

BEING SOCIAL WITHOUT SCREENS
Appropriate levels of feel-good neurochemicals are released in our brains when we are with our friends in person, allowing us to connect emotionally.

PLAYING MUSIC
Listening to music and playing musical instruments stimulates more brain areas than any other activity. You don't need to be gifted—you just need to listen or play!

WRITING ON PAPER
Our brains are highly stimulated through touch. Handwriting a letter, rather than typing, stimulates more neural pathways for healthy brain growth.

BEING CREATIVE WITH ART & DRAMA
Your imagination is like a muscle—it must be used and worked. Art and drama promote creativity and problem-solving skills, which help our brains develop.

GETTING ENOUGH SLEEP
Our brains need sleep. During sleep, the brain reorganizes information, regulates emotions, and repairs damaged cells. Sleep is essential for our brains to be their best.

BEING OUTSIDE IN NATURE
Nature is a natural stress reducer. It can increase our ability to focus, boost our mood, and perk us up when our brains are tired. Let's be outdoors as much as we can!

READING BOOKS
Reading helps develop the imagination, vocabulary, and critical thinking skills. It also helps develop empathy as we relate to the characters and their struggles.

HOW DO WE GET BETTER AT ANY SKILL OR ACTIVITY?

The longer we PRACTICE any activity, the better we get, and the easier it becomes.

Think about the first time you shot a basketball, kicked a soccer ball, swam on your own, or rode a bike. Think about when you could finally play a song on the piano or bake cookies all by yourself. These activities were awkward and even challenging at first, but they are easy now because you practiced and didn't give up. You strengthened your neural pathways.

HARD WORK REALLY PAYS OFF!

Practicing hard things gives our brains a workout. When we persevere with difficult tasks, our brains get stronger, and we develop grit. Then, when we get good at doing hard things, we will feel competent and more confident.

When we are ScreenStrong, we get comfortable doing hard things. Some days, we may feel like quitting, but we know what is important and are not afraid to stick to our goals even when they stretch us. **We will never regret standing up and working hard for something important. Furthermore, when we practice being different, we get better at that, too, which is a win.**

EXECUTIVE FUNCTIONING SKILLS

Doctors have discovered that certain activities can improve the brain's judgment center, also called the **executive center**—the area in the front part of our brains that helps us make good decisions.

When our executive center is healthy, it helps us with essential life skills called **executive functioning skills. These skills help us focus, solve problems, get along with others, and manage everyday life.**

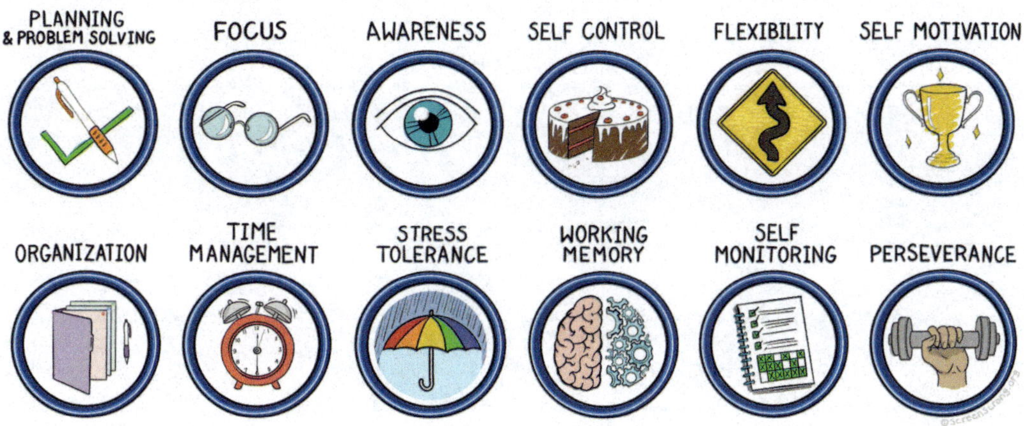

FOCUS AND ATTENTION

One of our most important brain skills is focusing on one task at a time. When we flood our brains with too much information, our attention spans shorten, and learning is harder.

HOW DO I PRACTICE EXECUTIVE FUNCTIONING SKILLS?

Executive functioning skills aren't something we're born with; we have to work on developing them on purpose. It's especially great to start learning these skills during childhood and adolescence. **Practice is key—the more we do them, the better we get.**

But here's the deal: if we don't take the chance to build up these skills early on, we might face some challenges later. **The good news? We are in charge of making our brains stronger.** Right now, we can do some simple things to boost the executive functioning part of our brains.

BE SCREENSTRONG & BUILD A STRONGER BRAIN!

SECTION 3
DOES SCREEN TIME CHANGE MY BRAIN?

"Scientists have discovered that too much screen time can harm areas of our brains. PURR-haps we need to rethink our screen habits and save our brains!"

Skippy, The ScreenStrong Cat

There have been some exciting advances in brain imaging technology. Years ago, CAT scans were the only picture you could take of a brain to give a rough idea if there was damage to the brain. Today, technology has moved to an advanced tool called **magnetic resonance imaging (MRI).** MRI is a medical tool that uses magnets and computer-generated radio waves to make detailed pictures of your body's organs and tissues.

It's as if we have a large, clear window to the brain. We can peer inside and see how the brain functions. **Researchers now have an accurate way to get more data about how certain activities change areas of the brain.**

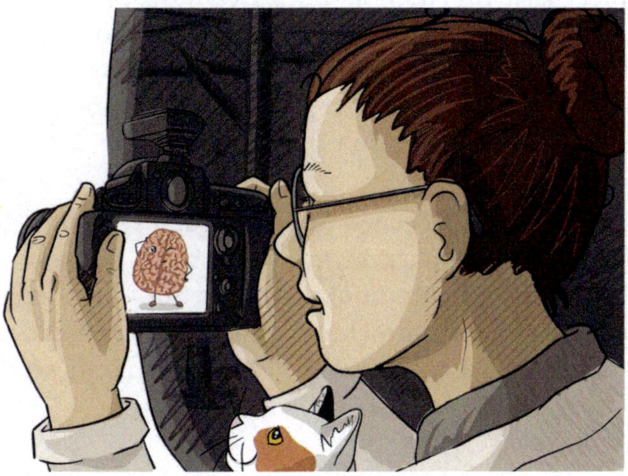

IMPACTS OF SCREENS ON BRAINS: THE SCIENCE

When we talk with our friends, read this book, play an instrument, or play soccer, we use multiple neurons from a wide area of our brains. Areas that control language, judgment, and imagination are highly involved and working together.

Interactive screen activities use limited regions of the brain. Stimulating screen overuse, especially of quick media, like short TikTok videos and video games, **overstimulates the reward center and understimulates the judgment center.**

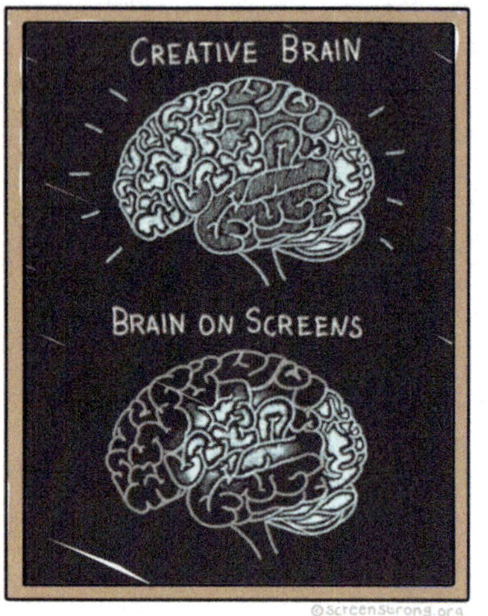

©screenstrong.org

LESS ACTIVE BRAINS

Scientists have found that when kids use screens a lot, their brains are less active in a critical area—the cortex or outer layer—that processes information. Because young brains are growing so fast and are highly sensitive to experiences, these findings raise concerns that **the brain may not develop properly with too much screen use.** Isn't that worrisome?

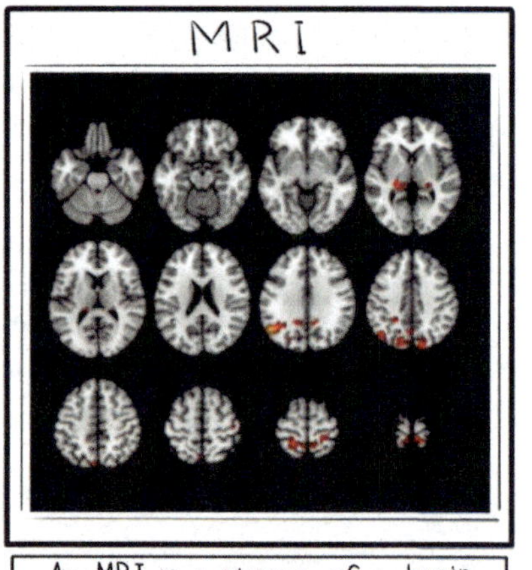

An MRI is a picture of a brain that helps doctors detect problems

©screenstrong.org

Doctors are concerned about this and recommend that families be careful. Dr. David R. Rosenberg, MD, says, "A brain hooked on the internet, phones, or tablets **looks like a brain hooked on heroin**—an addictive drug. There is a striking difference compared to healthy adolescents. The brain's processing center is not the same as a normal child." **This is serious stuff.**

THE ABCD BRAIN STUDY

Doctors are committed to learning more about young brains, so the National Institutes of Health funded the ABCD Study. This large study uses MRI tests and follows more than 11,000 children for ten years, starting around nine years old. Part of the study is designed to determine the **effect of too much screen time during preteen and teenage years.**

The researchers are discovering that young people with excessive screen time —more than seven hours a day—have changes in their brain structure. The **outer cortex—areas supporting decision-making, working memory, and self-control—is significantly understimulated,** which may indicate underdevelopment. They are finding significant structural changes in the brains of children as young as nine years old.

THEY SAW THE FOLLOWING RESULTS IN KIDS WHO WERE ON THEIR SCREENS TOO MUCH.

Lower cognitive (thinking) and language test scores were recorded for children who used screens for an excessive amount of time.

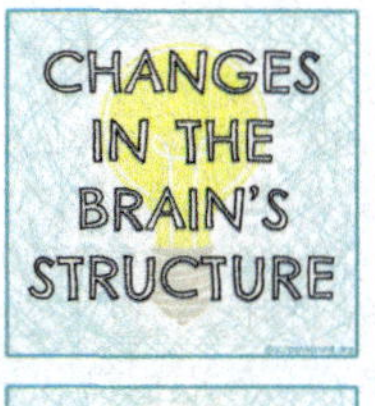

The part of the brain that should be full and thick in young people was shown to be much thinner in those who spent too much time on screens.

Lower crystallized intelligence (knowledge from prior learning) was found regarding language, general word and vocabulary knowledge, and reading comprehension for children overusing screens.

LESS SCREENS = MORE DEVELOPED BRAINS

This is a 3-D view of the left side of the brain, captured using a special MRI that looks at fiber connections between nerves on the surface, called white matter. The gray areas show the brain's normal surface and folds (called gyri).

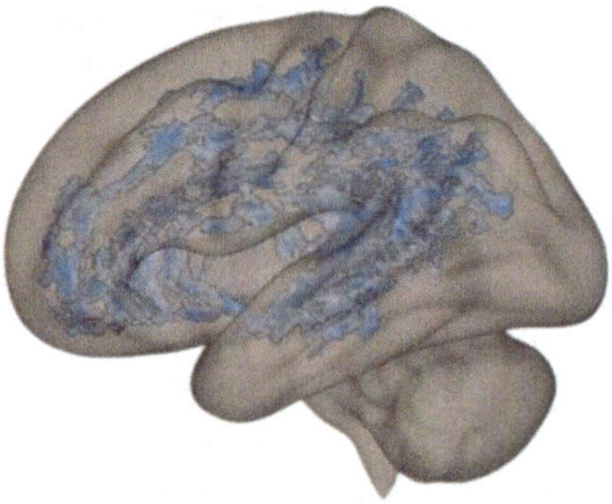

Dr. John S. Hutton, MD, MS, a pediatrician and clinical researcher, uses MRIs for his studies. In one study, he looked at how the level of digital media use (screen time) relates to the maturity and efficiency of nerve fibers in a group of preschool children aged 3 to 5 years old.

His study found that higher levels of screen time were associated with **less-developed** (which means slower and less efficient) white matter, as shown by the blue areas.

This relationship was found in many parts of the brain *(as the above picture from his study shows)*, especially in language, executive function, and reading. In this study, kids with more screen time also had lower scores on tests of these skills.

"The consistency of these brain findings involving young children and those involving teens suggests that there may be a cumulative impact of digital media use, which tends to increase with age. Thus, limiting screen time and encouraging healthy alternatives as early as possible make up a sound strategy to help children grow up healthy, well-adjusted, and successful in school and life. "

—Dr. John S. Hutton, MD, MS, pediatrician and clinical researcher

VIDEO GAMES TRAIN BRAINS

Did you know the first video games were created in the 1960s to train soldiers? These games were simple, text-based programs that simulated missile launches or air combat scenarios; the repetition helped soldiers prepare for battle.

Lt. Col. David Grossman, a former psychology professor at the United States Military Academy (West Point), has years of training soldiers in the U.S. Army and knows the science behind killing. He explains that it is difficult for a healthy human to pull the trigger and end someone's life unless that person has been desensitized and trained to kill. This is what he says about gaming:

"Kids playing brutal games have been taught to associate death and suffering with their popcorn and candy bars. We have millions of children who have been classically conditioned from their youngest days to take pleasure in human death and suffering. To them, at a deep, primal level, human death and suffering are a source of intense pleasure. What is the lasting impact of heavy gaming? Stunted social skills, aggression, and lack of self-restraint."

When gamers play a violent game and pull the trigger to shoot someone, they get a reward for a job well done. With repetition, their brains begin to think that killing is a good thing. After all, they did get a reward. This is called **classical conditioning**—training that creates a subconscious reaction—and it's hard to reverse. Over time, the line blurs between video game violence and real-life violence because the brain doesn't know the difference between the two. **Gamers can be desensitized to gore and violence, which can make them more aggressive in real life.**

WINDING UP, NOT DOWN

Screen time is very much like a stimulant drug, just like caffeine, nicotine, or even cocaine. It disrupts our nervous system, interrupting the signals between the brain and body. While scrolling, posting, fighting, strategizing, surviving, accumulating weapons, and running for our lives, our brains' judgment center (frontal cortex) shuts down, and the emotion center (limbic center) takes over. **We may think we are winding down, but the reality is that our brains are getting overstimulated and exhausted.**

THE OVERSTIMULATED BRAIN

Once the brain gets overexcited and agitated by screen use, we get irritated when we are interrupted. **The impulse control part of the brain is not working well.** If this happens too often, we get frustrated and overreact at the drop of a hat.

Here is an inside look at the malfunctions that happen in our brains when we overdo screens.

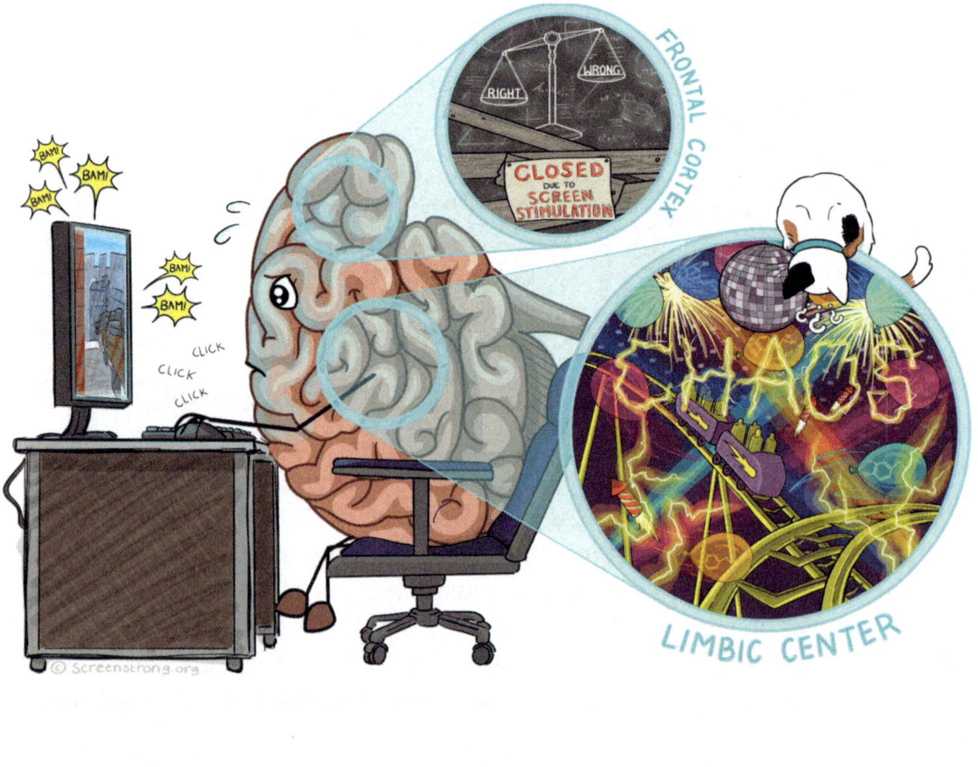

IS YOUR BRAIN GETTING SMALLER?

Dr. Victoria Dunckley, a medical doctor who discovered Electronic Screen Syndrome (ESS), works with kids just like you. She says,

"With screen overuse, the reward pathways get overdeveloped, and the other pathways and other parts of the brain are underdeveloped. We can actually see these in brain scans. We can see certain brain areas have atrophy or shrinkage; generally, the brain is less connected. ***Screen time causes a brain to be smaller and less connected."***

ELECTRONIC SCREEN SYNDROME

Our nervous system takes a hit when we text repeatedly or are on a video game for a long time. Our fight-or-flight system is stimulated, and this causes our brains to get revved up to the point where it is hard for us to control our tempers, adjust our moods, or pay attention. This is called **Electronic Screen Syndrome**. It is best to remove the screens causing the problem until the judgment center of the brain is more mature and connected.

Don't stress out.
Your 25th birthday will be here before you know it!

TWENTY-FIVE YEARS

Brain science indicates that it takes 25+ years for the judgment center of our brains to grow up. This is the part of our brains that is hurt the most by screen time. As a result, kids might find themselves doing things that are a bit unpredictable or risky, even when they don't plan to. Dr. Dunckley says, "That's why having parents or other caring adults is super important to help kids make big decisions. What makes the most sense is to delay exposure to harmful screens for now."

DON'T HURT YOUR BRAIN

Spending a lot of time playing video games and being on smartphones may seem okay initially, but it does more harm than good in the long run.

Our screen time can't provide everything we need to build a healthy brain and help us understand, engage in, and enjoy the natural world.

Let's make sure we develop healthy habits in our lives so we can have the healthiest brains possible!

SAVE THE BRAINS!

If this all seems scary, don't worry. We have control over how we spend our time, and we CAN fix the problem. By putting screens down as often as possible and investing our time in healthier activities, we can give our brains what they need to reverse the problems with screen dependency and addiction.

LIMIT SCREEN TIME
Trade all those screen hours for healthy hobbies instead.

EXERCISE
Exercising at least 60 minutes a day is necessary for your brain to grow and stay healthy.

CONNECTIONS
Stay connected to parents, caring adults, and good friends.

SLEEP
It is essential to get at least nine hours of sleep each night. That's a lot!

INTERESTING ACTIVITIES
Our brains need to have a variety of healthy activities to keep all the neurons talking to each other.

CAN YOU REMEMBER?

1. What are the cells called that connect the areas of the brain?

- ☐ Connector cells
- ☐ Neurons
- ☐ Jail cells
- ☐ Stem cells

2. When is your brain finished developing?

- ☐ After your 5th birthday
- ☐ Not until you are in your mid-20s
- ☐ When you can finally beat *League of Legends*
- ☐ Once you are a grandparent

3. Which of the following will make your brain stronger? Select all that apply.

- ☐ Exercising
- ☐ Doing art and playing music
- ☐ Watching YouTube for two hours
- ☐ Getting nine hours of sleep every night

WHAT CAN YOU DO RIGHT NOW?

- ☐ Make your bed every morning.
- ☐ Get a job in your neighborhood. Jobs help you build executive functioning skills. They'll also allow you to make a little extra money, too!
- ☐ Plan non-tech times to hang out with your friends. Invite them to shoot hoops, play board games, or make pizza together.
- ☐ Get outside in nature more. Make plans to meet your friends after school on a playing field or in a nearby park to throw a Frisbee, shoot hoops, or walk together.
- ☐ Sign up for music and/or art chapters with a friend.

NOTES

CHAPTER TWO

SO WHAT'S THE BIG DEAL WITH SCREENS?

CHAPTER 2: INTRODUCTION
SO WHAT'S THE BIG DEAL WITH SCREENS?

Welcome to Chapter Two.

Have you ever wondered why you crave more screen time?

In this chapter, you'll learn the biggest secret to understanding why screens are irresistible and addictive. It has to do with a brain chemical called dopamine.

Remember those electrochemical signals we discussed in Chapter One? Well, dopamine is one of them. When you engage in specific screen activities, your brain releases a hefty dose of dopamine. This dopamine causes our brain to crave screens more.

You're about to learn what screen addiction is and why some screen activities are more addictive than others. And you'll discover how scientists work their magic behind the scenes to capture our attention.

There is so much more to the screen discussion than we ever imagined.

In this chapter, look out for the answers to the following questions:

1. *What activities release healthy amounts of dopamine?*
2. *How many hours does the average teen spend on a screen every day?*
3. *How do tech companies keep you hooked on your screens?*

Let's pay better attention to how screens hook us so we won't get hooked!

Lydia

"There is a chemical in your brain that makes you fall in love with your screen? That's unFUR-tunate!"

Skippy, The ScreenStrong Cat

WHAT IS DOPAMINE?

Let's start with the basics. Why are screens so much fun? The answer can be summed up in one word: **DOPAMINE.**

Dopamine is like the brain's happy messenger. It tells the reward center that something feels good. **It's the reason we feel pleasure and satisfaction.**

Dopamine also motivates us to keep doing things that make us feel good, like eating or exercising—things we need to do to stay healthy. But here's the catch: too much or too little dopamine can cause big problems.

Dopamine is like the main character in addiction. Too much dopamine is released in the brain when unhealthy choices are made, like drinking alcohol, gambling, or using drugs. And you know what? Using screens too much also floods our brains with dopamine. It's all about dopamine.

HOW DOPAMINE WORKS

Our brains release normal amounts of dopamine when we eat, exercise, and do other activities that help us stay alive. Dopamine is also released in our brains when we solve a complex math problem, hit a home run, or get asked to the school dance. The brain says, "Wow! That was fun. Let's keep doing that." Dopamine makes us feel good and prompts us to do the activity again.

With the **right amount** of dopamine, we feel happy, motivated, and focused. We feel a sense of satisfaction and can accomplish many things.

TOO MUCH DOPAMINE

When we get too much dopamine, it can disrupt the balance in our brain's reward system.

At first, when our brains are filled with happy chemicals, we feel amazing. But then, **the good feelings fade, and our dopamine levels drop.** That's when we start feeling tired, moody, and sad. **Feeling sad makes us want to do the activity that makes us happy again.** So we continue, and the cycle starts over.

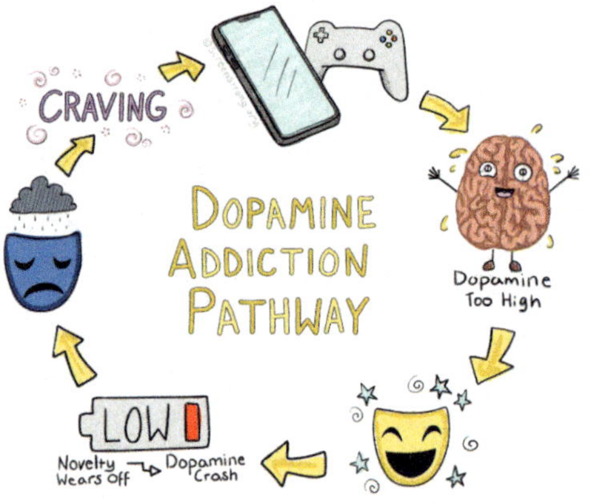

Our brains learn to enjoy that happy feeling, and soon, we can't stop—we get stuck in an addiction cycle. **Screen activities are designed to give us a HUGE dopamine rush**—way more than healthy activities. Now our brains want that big dopamine surge from screens, even if we're not having that much fun anymore. It's like our brains get hooked on screens.

"Over time, gaming floods your brain with dopamine, making the real world feel dull. The game starts playing you—it becomes your reality. When the high fades, you feel low, so you game again to chase the rush."

—Adam Brooker, former gamer

THE RIGHT AMOUNT OF DOPAMINE

Dopamine is beneficial for us in balanced, natural amounts, known as our baseline. We stay healthy by engaging in enjoyable activities that provide the right, natural doses of dopamine. Examples include spending time in nature, hanging out with friends, exercising, or learning to play a new song.

How can you tell if you have the right amount? When we do healthy activities, we feel better afterward. Conversely, if we engage in activities that produce excessive dopamine, we feel good at first but tend to feel worse afterward. It's all about finding that healthy balance of dopamine.

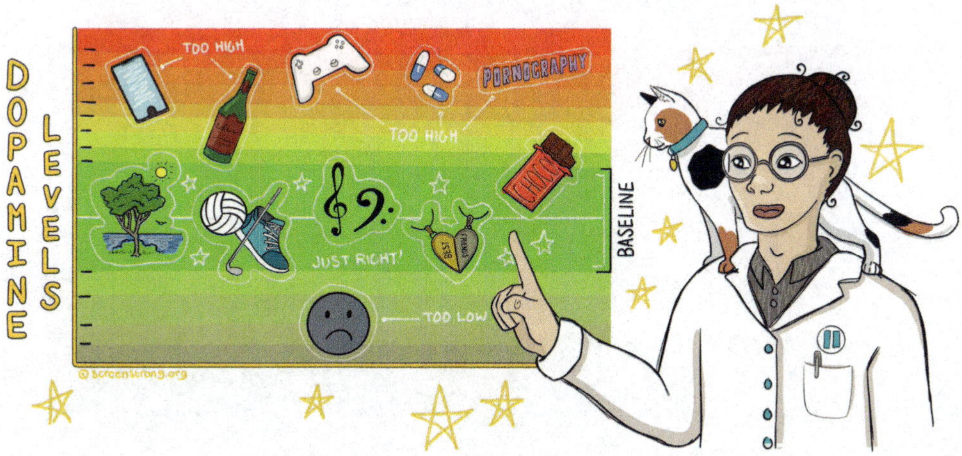

THE PROBLEM WITH HIGH DOPAMINE

Have you ever felt like one of your favorite video games is starting to get boring, or have you felt irritable after too much screen time? This happens because our brains go through something called **tolerance**. Understanding tolerance can be a bit tricky, so let's break it down into a few straightforward steps:

1. The brain gets flooded with dopamine from interactive screen activities like playing video games or overusing social media.
2. The brain gets tricked into thinking that high dopamine levels are normal, so now the rush doesn't feel that great anymore.
3. The brain now interprets the rush as a standard baseline and craves more dopamine to feel normal or good again.

EFFECTS OF TOLERANCE

EFFECT #1

Less satisfaction with healthy doses of dopamine: Normal activities no longer produce enough dopamine to create a good feeling.

EFFECT #2

A drive to seek out more thrilling versions of the activity: More violent video games, more edgy content on social media, or a different high-dopamine-producing activity altogether is needed to get the same good feeling.

OVER TIME, THINGS GET WORSE

We try to stop the screen activity, but our natural dopamine levels no longer make us happy. Things like going outside and hanging out with our families aren't as fun as they used to be. So we become sad. This sadness creates a **craving** for more screen activity. Our **tolerance** keeps rising because our brains can never get enough. This is how we get stuck in the screen addiction trap.

SECTION 2
WHY DO I CRAVE MY SCREENS?

> "Scientists work hard—using PURR-suasive design—to keep our eyes glued to our screens."
>
> *Skippy, The ScreenStrong Cat*

When we understand why we use screens, we have a better chance of having a healthy relationship with them.

EXPLORE SOME COMMON REASONS YOU ARE **DRAWN TO YOUR SCREENS**

TO ESCAPE
Life is kind of hard right now at home, and you want to zone out on your screen to avoid thinking about the problems.

TO BE CHALLENGED
Your game provides a challenging environment for you; maybe you're not being challenged enough in school.

TO WIN
A part of your brain gets a natural high when you win. You love this feeling of triumph. You are very competitive. The game is fulfilling your need to compete.

TO AVOID ANXIETY
You may pick up your screen when you are anxious and trying to avoid stress, but screen time only makes you more anxious and stressed in the long run.

TO REPLACE ATHLETICS
You didn't make the school team this year, you moved, or sports just got too hard for you. Now you have a lot of extra time on your hands, and your video game has become your new "sport."

TO BE CREATIVE
You believe you're being creative online; however, playing a game someone else created is not being creative. Building something in real life is a much better choice.

TO FEEL BETTER ABOUT YOURSELF
You don't feel that good about yourself, but on your game, people think you are pretty great. You feel like you have a group of friends who respect you.

TO ESCAPE BULLIES AT SCHOOL
You choose gaming because bullies at school hurt you. You have more control over your game world. If someone is mean to you in the game, you can choose not to talk to them.

TO FEEL NORMAL
Just like a fish doesn't know what water is, sometimes we're unaware that we're immersed in the virtual world. We don't know why we reach for our screens; it feels so normal that we don't realize we're doing it.

TO FILL BOREDOM
You pick up your screen because you're bored, and your brain craves dopamine.

TO AVOID BEING LONELY
You are turning to screens because you are alone, but your screen only makes you feel more lonely.

TO FEEL ACCOMPLISHED
You are gaming because you feel a strong sense of accomplishment when you play.

TO FIND PURPOSE
You're trying to find purpose on your screen instead of in real life. A lack of purpose makes you feel bad and leads to bad choices.

PASSIVE VS. INTERACTIVE

Many years ago, entertainment technology was fun to play, but it was also more simple. Kids played arcade games, and **once the quarters were gone, the gaming session was over.** Kids left and did something else like ride their bikes home with friends. It was more difficult to get addicted.

Television shows, another passive screen activity, were usually limited to 30-minute episodes. There was a week between episodes, so viewers had time to anticipate and discuss their favorite shows, fostering a sense of community around shared viewing experiences. Video streaming services that are popular today didn't exist.

Those screens were passive; they had a natural stopping point, unlike the interactive screens we have today that require constant responses from us. **Very few healthy hobbies will allow you to play for 10+ hours at a time.** The immersive nature of entertainment screens, along with the absence of natural stopping points, makes them a high risk for addiction.

HOW SOCIAL MEDIA AND VIDEO GAME COMPANIES MAKE BANK

Tech companies discovered that the longer people stay on their screen platform, the more money the company makes through advertising and in-app and in-game purchases. They see our attention as a resource that can make them rich—but only if they can capture it. Consequently, they invest a lot of money to find ways to grab and keep our attention.

As video games and other screen activities evolved, consumer technology companies learned that they could boost profits if people spent more time on their screen "products."

To keep customers' attention 24/7, these companies hire special scientists called **attention engineers** to make their platforms more fun and difficult to leave—they make them addictive.

For centuries, scientists have been fascinated with why humans do things. They studied hard and discovered three psychological drivers that motivate us to do what we do: our drive for **pleasure**, **social connection** (and fear of social rejection), and **rewards**. This knowledge has been turned into a whole field of screen science called **persuasive design**.

DO TECH COMPANIES WANT US TO STAY OFF SCREENS? NOPE.

Social media and video game companies aren't concerned if we give up the baseball team or piano lessons to devote more time to posting or gaming on their platforms. They're not bothered if we feel anxious or sad or act out when our parents limit our screen time. **These companies want us to abandon other activities to grab ALL our attention**—after all, that's how they rake in the money. They'd be thrilled if we spent every waking minute on our screens.

We don't have to get caught up in persuasive design. **We can choose how we spend our time and where we direct our attention.** Understanding what's happening behind the scenes on our screens and the power of persuasive design makes it possible for us to make better choices. Let's look at how screens act like magnets that pull us in.

"The reason youth are struggling is not a lack of willpower or a shortage of parental concern. The reason is that consumer technology corporations are treating our kids as a resource to be controlled through the powerful psychology of persuasive design."

—Richard Freed, PhD, psychologist and author of *Wired Child: Reclaiming Childhood in a Digital Age*

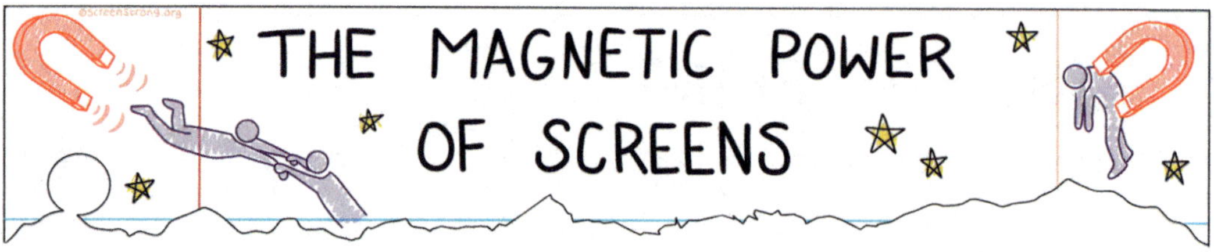

Have you ever been in the middle of a video game when your mom calls you for dinner, and you get mad because you don't want to leave the game? Has a phone notification triggered you to look at your phone even while you were with a group of friends? Have you ever slept with your phone in your bed?

The **neuroscientists** working behind our favorite apps and games have mastered the art of capturing our attention and pulling us from things we should be doing instead. They use scientific techniques to hook our attention. Warning: even when we understand these techniques, we still find ourselves unable to resist their power to keep us glued to our screens.

The following three elements work together deep in our subconscious to shape decisions that favor choosing screen activities over spending time doing anything else.

We crave quick rewards. Screen activities offer instant rewards and gratification, quickly activating the brain's pleasure center.

The fear of being left out of our social groups is strong. We crave social interaction, but time on phones and video games provides a weak and false sense of social connection.

Predictable rewards are powerful. The consistent screen rewards we get reinforce the behavior of choosing screen activities over time with people.

PERSUASIVE DESIGN: HOW TO CONTROL HUMAN BEHAVIOR

How do our screens make us choose phones or video games over having dinner with our family? It is not by accident; it is biology. By combining the following three elements, our behavior can be effectively controlled.

The formula for persuasive design is **Behavior** = **Motivation** + **Ability** + **Triggers**. Let's examine how each element is used to take advantage of our brains.

Make it fun. We are motivated to seek pleasure and social connections and to avoid the pain of social rejection. Social media and gaming make us think we are connecting. Scientists know that if they can make you feel connected, they can get you hooked.

Make it easy. People instinctively choose easy over difficult things. It takes a lot more work to learn something new, so screens are designed to be easy to use, even for 4-year-olds. We are more likely to do simple tasks over complex ones. Given the choice between playing on a screen or doing math homework, we will likely choose screen entertainment.

Make it irresistible. Triggers grab our attention and prompt immediate action. A doorbell is a perfect example of a trigger. Out of curiosity, we stop what we are doing and answer the door, just as screen notifications redirect our focus.

Tech companies know the power of triggers, so they use them and make them simple and irresistible. It's no accident that we find it so hard to resist the powerful magnetic pull of our devices.

Let's learn more about how immersive screens—tablets, smartphones, and video games—are designed and how companies are working hard to keep us hooked.

WHY WE CAN'T PUT DOWN OUR GAME

Our brains naturally gravitate towards activities that promise the highest dopamine rewards. So video game science uses a two-step process to keep us hooked on our games:

Step One: Grab our attention. They employ attention-grabbing hooks to get our attention. These can range from vibrant colors and realistic graphics to catchy music and sounds—all designed to captivate our senses and draw us in.

Step Two: Keep our attention. Next, they utilize attention-sustaining hooks in the form of rewards to keep our attention. These hooks tap into the intricacies of how the human brain processes and craves rewards. The timing of these rewards and the anticipation of the next prize play crucial roles in determining how much dopamine is released and how closely we remain focused on the screen. It's a strategic science designed to keep us hooked and engaged.

Gaming perfectly combines challenges, competition, the feeling of belonging, escape, fantasy, and freedom.

Gamers feel so much excitement when they game because dopamine is released when they play.

Gamers get excited just talking or thinking about the game, not only when they are playing but also when they are watching others play and when they are away from their games. They feel gaming is their life purpose. But hold on, are gamers in control of the games, or are the games controlling them?

WE FOCUS ON WHAT GIVES US REWARDS, EVEN FAKE ONES

Scientists know they can get us to focus on meaningless tasks if they reward us correctly. The value of the reward itself doesn't matter at all. In fact, it can be as silly as a fake coin, and we will still skip dinner, time with family, or baseball practice to get it.

REWARD HOOKS THAT KEEP US PLAYING

Rewarding Your Progress: unlocking new levels, receiving tokens, obtaining hard-to-get objects

Including Surprises: never knowing when we will find incentives such as hidden treasure chests

Changing the Reward Schedule: making rewards easy to get at first but harder over time

Punishing Avoidance: losing rewards when not playing consistently and incentivizing frequent returns

Can you think of a time when you fell for these hooks? They make it so hard to stop! No one can resist these addictive design elements.

THE DARKER SIDE OF GAMES

The video game industry is a $180 billion industry (yes, billion with a B) and it brings in more money than Hollywood and professional sports combined. How do video game companies make all this money? They know how to lure us in with free games, capture our attention, and then entice us to spend real money.

Even if a game is free to play, it uses in-game purchases like character customizations and subscriptions (skins, battle passes, loot, etc.). Some gamers steal from their parents using their credit cards without permission to buy online products. Some people—even adults—spend a lot of money on these in-game purchases and can't stop. Others get caught in online gambling addictions through their video games and other apps.

Additional dark elements of video games include exposure to online predators and inappropriate and harmful content. In addition, violence in video games has been linked to real-life aggression. There is much more going on in a video game than we may realize.

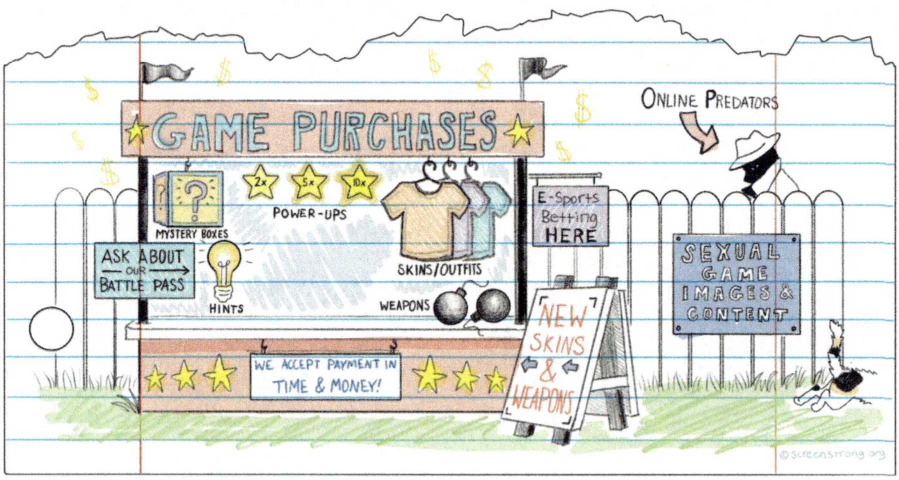

MICROTRANSACTIONS
$93 billion is spent on microtransactions like buying skins in a game. That is eight times more than is spent purchasing the games themselves.

IN-GAME PURCHASES
In 2020, the average *Fortnite* player spent over $102/yr on in-game purchases, and the average *League of Legends* player spent over $92/yr.

ONLINE PREDATORS
Predators target multi-player games and forums like Discord. They can trick and harm kids because the their real identities are hidden.

E-SPORTS & GAMBLING
E-sports programs have popped up at colleges nationwide and encourage young people to gamble.

HOW GAMING TAKES OVER OUR LIVES

How do smart kids like us fall into the trap of screen addiction?

Spending all our time on video games can quickly become a habit. How can a video game habit turn into an addiction?

1. SILLY GAMES
Gaming starts innocently with access to meaningless silly content. Parents attempt to set time limits.

3. CONFLICT AT HOME
We argue with our parents over game time and drop out of sports and other hobbies. Games are making us stressed out.

5. WE ARE STUCK
We want to stop, but we can't. We have to play more to get the same good feeling. We are losing sleep and friends. We don't know what our life purpose is outside of gaming.

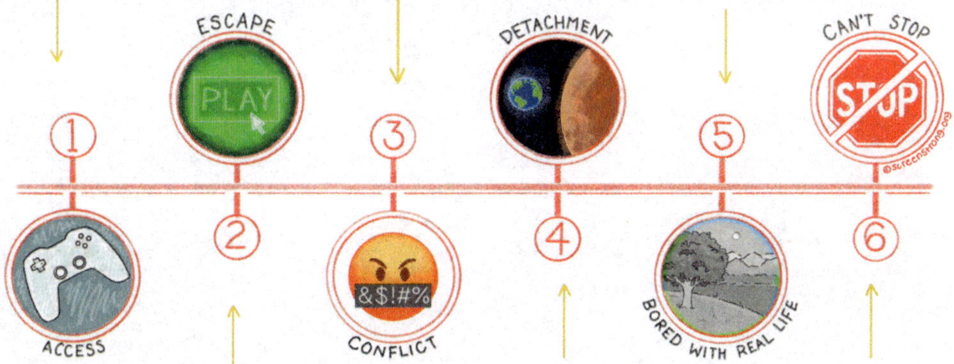

2. MORE MATURE GAMES
We get into more violent games like *Fortnite*. We are exposed to violence, strangers, foul language, and dark topics in games that are rated too high for us. We begin to play more than our parents want and gaming becomes an escape.

4. DETACHMENT FROM FAMILY
We spend more time with the game than with family. We feel sad but gaming doesn't help like it once did. We begin to lie to cover up our gaming habits.

6. ADDICTION STARTS
We have lost control over our habit. We think we can stop, but we can't. We feel depressed and don't know how to get out of the trap.

"The virtual world becomes your reality, and the real world becomes an inconvenience. If you don't get bored after 30 minutes of game play and walk away, you may be headed for trouble like I was."

—Adam Brooker, former gamer

WHY WE CAN'T PUT DOWN OUR PHONES

Do you feel panicky—like you will not be able to survive—if you lose your phone? You're not alone. Similar to video games, our smartphones are designed to captivate our attention, occupy our time, and keep us emotionally attached to them.

"I'M IN LOVE!"

Using MRI technology, scientists explain why we feel such a strong attachment to smartphones. When we engage with our phones, we experience the same emotions as if we are in love.

MRI tests show that the same brain area lights up when we see a loved one and when we see our phones. This profound attachment to a phone is linked to the release of dopamine and oxytocin. **Oxytocin** is called the "love hormone" because it helps us bond with others. It also makes us feel a sense of love towards our phones! Is that a good thing?

SMARTPHONE TRAPS

Smartphones have good uses, but it's essential to understand how they can quickly hook us and make us feel trapped.

Just like video games, smartphones are loaded with these persuasive design traps:

- **NOVELTY OF CONTENT**
  Our brains are programmed to love new things. There is always something new on our phones to steal our attention away from what we are doing.
- **BRIGHT COLORS**
  The bright colors on smartphones are there to drive dopamine up and make phones irresistible. People will use their phones less when phones are set to grayscale. It is easy to change the setting and what a great idea!
- **SENSE OF BELONGING**
  We need people to like us; everyone has this need. Social media and online interactions trick us into thinking people care when they don't.
- **UNLIMITED CONTENT**
  A smartphone offers no shortage of entertainment, good and bad. It's an endless scroll. No one needs entertainment 24/7. Our brains need a break.
- **EASE OF USE**
  The tech on a phone is so easy a 4-year-old can use it. No training is required.
- **CAUSE AND EFFECT**
  Have you ever watched your little brother or sister play with the light switch? They turn it on and off over and over again. We are all fascinated by cause and effect, and phones use lots of buttons and features to keep us hooked.
- **SURPRISES**
  Phone notifications are like little gifts to open, but they are triggers that trap us.
- **FEAR OF MISSING OUT (FOMO)**
  The fear of missing out on something makes us worry and pick up our phones. "Did they have a party last night without me? Let me check my phone."
- **LIKES AND TAGS**
  We get a false sense of belonging if we get enough likes and tags. They make us feel important. We are hoping to be famous one day soon.
- **NOTIFICATION TRIGGERS**
  When our phone alerts us to pay attention to it, that message is hard to ignore.

ALGORITHMS

We may think we control our screen content, but we don't. The companies that make the app or game decide what we see online.

Algorithms are the way companies determine what the user sees. They track every time we click and like something, put it in a big data file, and then use that information to customize our feeds. They even know how long we hover over something.

We may think we're in control of what ends up in our feeds or the next streaming video, but we're not; every feed is unique to the person on it. Much money is spent on making algorithms more effective. Tech companies know they'll make more money by creating the most personal flow of content. The more personalized a cue or trigger is, the more attractive it becomes—and the more it controls our screen behavior.

Content that is novel or disgusting both captures and retains attention better than emotionally neutral content. We can't look away, and we become anxious.

Anxiety prompts a focus on the negative idea that triggered the anxiety to begin with. The user now searches for more of the negative topics.

More searches about a stressful topic lead to confusion as the algorithm keeps serving up similar topics. When surrounded by a community of anxious people feeding on inaccurate information in the virtual world, the user often falls into despair. *(See Lydia's story).*

SOCIAL MEDIA: NOT DESIGNED FOR TEENAGERS

1. **Wasted Time:** It isn't easy to control the amount of time we spend on social media apps. They are all designed to keep us hooked. Before long, a few minutes turn into a few hours, and we have lost opportunities to do more meaningful activities.

2. **Comparison:** Social media can significantly impact our self-esteem. We see that perfect photos get the most likes, so we feel we must look perfect, too. When we compare ourselves to others, we are never happy. This can lead to needless feelings of self-doubt, inadequacy, and even depression.

3. **Unwanted Content:** We cannot control or avoid harmful and inappropriate content coming our way on social media. We will see it even if we try to avoid it.

Snapchat:

- Features disappearing content
- Encourages overuse by pressuring users to share and achieve a high streak score
- Encourages self-criticism due to constant picture-taking

Instagram:

- Impacts self-esteem when we see that perfectly posed photos gain the most attention
- Has very limited privacy controls, offering an inadequate private account feature
- Permits cyberbullying and explicit content

TikTok:

- Features short videos that spike dopamine, making this the most addictive app
- Encourages high engagement that can lead to physical and mental health problems
- Has data collection practices that put privacy at risk

SECTION 3
WHAT IS SCREEN ADDICTION?

> "It's now proven that video games and social media are addictive activities. Oh no! I like to sit in front of my computer and watch the mouse. PURR-haps, it's time we all get some new hobbies."
>
> *Skippy, The ScreenStrong Cat*

You might be wondering why there's so much fuss about screen time. After all, video games and social media seem harmless, right? Wrong. Screen activities are intentionally designed to be addictive. Let's start with some definitions.

What is addiction? Addiction is a powerful **craving** to do something hard to **control**, even when it has harmful **consequences** for ourselves or others. Addiction is a disorder of brain chemistry and involves an imbalance of the brain's feel-good chemical, dopamine.

What is screen addiction? Instead of a simple healthy increase in dopamine, screen activities can cause dopamine to flood the reward pathway more than natural rewards do. **Problems start when school, hobbies, and relationships are neglected because too much time is spent on screens.** Additional signs of screen addiction include physical and emotional imbalances and the inability to stop even after many attempts.

Social media and video games are among the most addictive screen activities. **Screen addiction destroys lives just like other addictions do.**

How screen addiction compares to smoking.

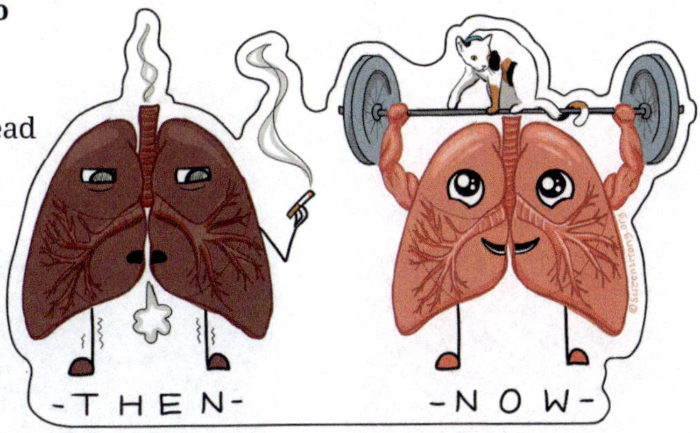

In the past, smoking was a widespread activity; even teens smoked. Surprisingly, doctors believed that smoking was fine, even beneficial. However, as time went on, people began experiencing health issues. Eventually, doctors realized the effects smoking had on many parts of the body, including the lungs.

Unfortunately, many people suffered and died before the public understood the risks of smoking. Once the public became educated about the dangers of smoking, people were empowered to make more informed decisions about their health.

The same thing is happening today with screens. Unfortunately, kids and teens are the unknowing test subjects of the screen experiment. They are getting hurt the worst. As more research emerges, **doctors realize screen overuse causes more harm than good to our brains and mental health.**

It's time for a change. With this new knowledge, we can shift how we think about screens. Just like smoking, **knowing the facts** allows us to make healthier choices.

REVIEW the following list of warning signs. Are any of them familiar?

WHAT ARE THE EFFECTS OF SCREEN OVERUSE?

Screen time is a solitary activity that keeps us **isolated and detached** from people in real life. Staying connected to our families and friends is necessary to stay mentally well.

Your future health will be determined by the influences and experiences you are exposed to now. **Harmful content**—unhealthy and dangerous subject matter—can hurt mental health.

Unhealthy and dangerous screen activities can lead to **depression** (sadness) **and anxiety** (worry). Spending too much time on a screen also makes us stressed. Chronic stress makes us sick.

More screen time means more sitting and less movement, which can lead to many **health problems**—eye problems, obesity, diabetes, & exhaustion.

Screen activities take so much time and provide so much **unhealthy dopamine** that it is hard to focus on school and be motivated to participate in meaningful hobbies.

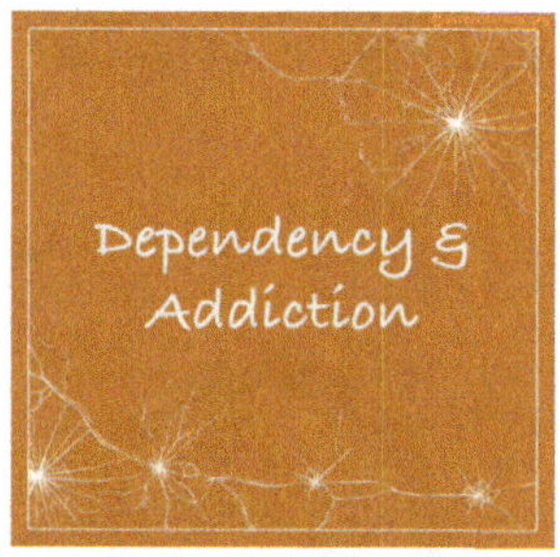

Video games, social media, and smartphones raise dopamine levels. Too much dopamine can lead to cravings, dependency, and even **screen addiction**.

HOW MUCH IS TOO MUCH?

Have you ever been on a video game or social media for what felt like a few minutes, but it turned out to be two hours? You are not alone. The big question today is how much time is just right for us to spend on entertainment screens.

Screen time has a way of taking over all of our free time.

The more we are on screens, the less time we have for mandatory activities that help us grow and stay healthy.

Look at the chart on the right—it shows what a balanced life could be like. But when we spend too much time on screens, we miss out on all the important stuff. We only have 24 hours a day, so we need to make sure we use it well.

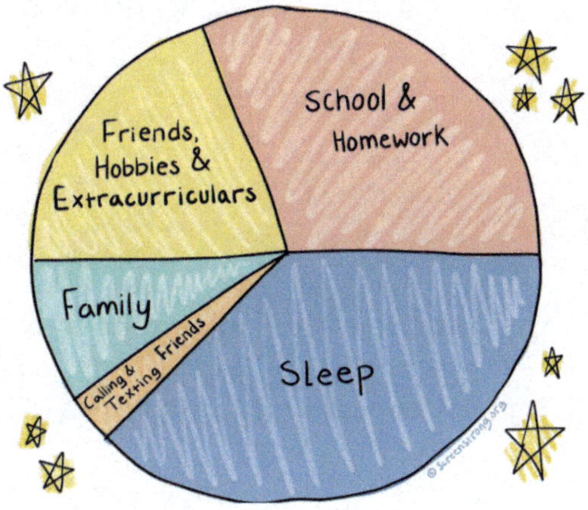

The average teen spends nine hours a day on a device. That adds up to more than **16,000 hours from 8th to 12th grade**. Imagine all the cool things you could do with that time instead of being on a screen—things like hanging out with family and friends or trying out awesome activities or new hobbies.

ATTENTION ENGINEERS WANT OUR 16,000 HOURS

Achieving true expertise in any skill takes about 10,000 hours of practice.

Imagine how good you could be at music, art, sports, science, or whatever you love after 16,000 hours of practice.

You could be one of the best in the world!

ARE YOU GETTING IN OVER YOUR HEAD?

CHECK ALL THAT APPLY TO YOU:

- [ ] You spend more and more time on a video game and/or smartphone every day.
- [ ] You play or scroll for long periods of time.
- [ ] You play or scroll to escape a problem or for excitement.
- [ ] You sacrifice social and extracurricular activities to be on a screen.
- [ ] You play a game or use your smartphone instead of doing homework.
- [ ] Over time, as screen activities get dull, you need different games and apps to get the same good feelings.
- [ ] You get sad or worried when you get off your game or smartphone.
- [ ] You try to get off screens or just cut down on screen time, but you can't.
- [ ] Your screen time is causing conflicts with your parents and friends, and you are losing interest in activities you used to like.

If you checked **two or more of the warning signs** for screen dependency, consider taking an extended break from video games and social media. It's time to **get back into some of your other hobbies** and give your brain a chance to **rest and reset.**

CAN YOU REMEMBER?

1. Which of the following activities release healthy amounts of dopamine? Check all that apply.

- ☐ Spending time with friends
- ☐ Playing a video game for an hour
- ☐ Running for exercise
- ☐ Consuming illegal drugs

2. How many hours does the average teen spend on a screen every day?

- ☐ Less than one hour
- ☐ Five hours
- ☐ Nine hours
- ☐ Too many hours to count

3. How do companies keep you hooked on screens?

- ☐ By creating apps that cause the brain to release excessive amounts of dopamine
- ☐ By changing the rewards you get and making them more exciting
- ☐ By using color and music to make things look new and different
- ☐ All of the above

WHAT CAN YOU DO RIGHT NOW?

- ☐ Make a list of activities you already do that produce healthy amounts of dopamine.
- ☐ Ask your parents to get you a talk/text phone instead of a smartphone.
- ☐ Turn off the color on all your screens this week (turn it to grayscale in the settings).
- ☐ Make a list of new hobbies, things you used to enjoy and could start doing again.
- ☐ Set your alarm to limit screen time to under 2 hours a day.
- ☐ Stop playing video games. Focus when you are in school and doing homework.
- ☐ Talk with three friends about what you learned in this chapter.
- ☐ Ask your parents for a family meeting to gather ideas on how to reduce EVERYONE'S daily screen use and spend more time together as a family.

NOTES

CHAPTER THREE

PHYSICAL: YOU'LL HAVE A STRONGER BODY

CHAPTER 3: INTRODUCTION
PHYSICAL: YOU'LL HAVE A STRONGER BODY

Welcome to Chapter Three.

Great job getting through the first two chapters!

You've learned how screens affect your brain and how addiction works. But screens don't just change how we think—they can also impact how we feel, grow, and connect with others.

Too much screen time can cause real physical issues like poor posture, back pain, and eye strain. It can also make us less active, which isn't great for staying healthy. Screens can even stress us out, mess with our emotions, and make us anxious.

In this chapter, you'll learn how to handle stress, avoid physical problems caused by screens, and make better choices when it comes to screen use. Plus, we'll cover the importance of sleep—it's how your brain recharges to keep you sharp and feeling great.

Watch for these questions:

1. *What is the 20-20-20 rule, and how can it help your eyes?*
2. *What's the fight-or-flight response, and how does stress trigger it?*
3. *How many hours of sleep do you need every night to be at your best?*

Let's dig in and figure out how to get stronger—mind, body, and soul!

Adam

"Chronic stress is caused by spending too much time on screens. And that's not a tall TAIL!"

Skippy, The ScreenStrong Cat

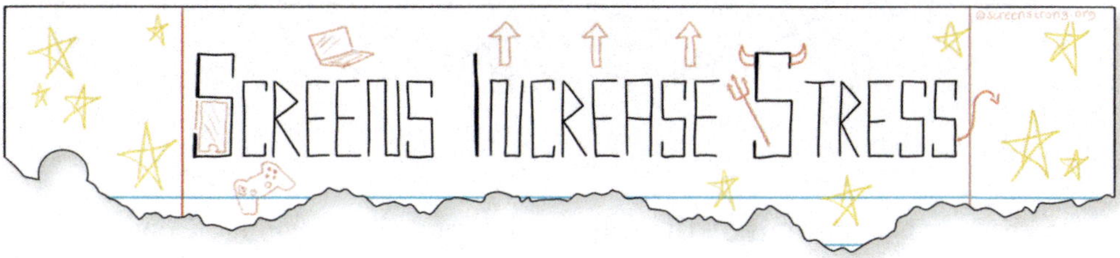

What is stress?

Stress is the brain's natural reaction to worry or frustration, helping us respond to challenges. While everyone faces stress, it becomes a problem when there's too much of it, and our bodies don't have a chance to rest and recover. The rapid evolution of technology has reached a point where our brains struggle to keep up with the constant stimulation from screens. When we're bombarded by endless content on our screens, our brains can get stressed out. Surprisingly, our brains treat this "screen stress" like it handles stress in real life—it can't tell the difference between the two.

INTRODUCING THE AMYGDALA

Think of the **amygdala** as a **tiny fire alarm in our brains,** about one inch in size. Its important role is to sound the alarm and **take charge of our brains when it senses potential danger or stress.** This little powerhouse interprets everything we see and hear, all in the name of keeping us safe. Nestled within the limbic system, the amygdala can take over and influence how we respond to stressful situations.

The amygdala gets activated by the following types of situations or content:

- Dangerous, violent, painful, or deadly situations
- Unfamiliar, novel (new or unusual), or gross content
- Emotionally charged or exciting activities

Spending just 20 minutes playing a violent video game can fire up the amygdala and cause a stress response.

THE STRESS RESPONSE

When something scary happens, the amygdala gets ready to protect us. Thus, it quickly revs up the body to fight or run away—hence the term **fight-flight**.

This physical reaction occurs in response to a perceived harmful attack, a virtual threat, or an actual physical threat to survival.

When a threat happens, the amygdala signals the adrenal glands—near the kidneys—to release stress hormones to take action.

INTRODUCING TWO STRESS HORMONES

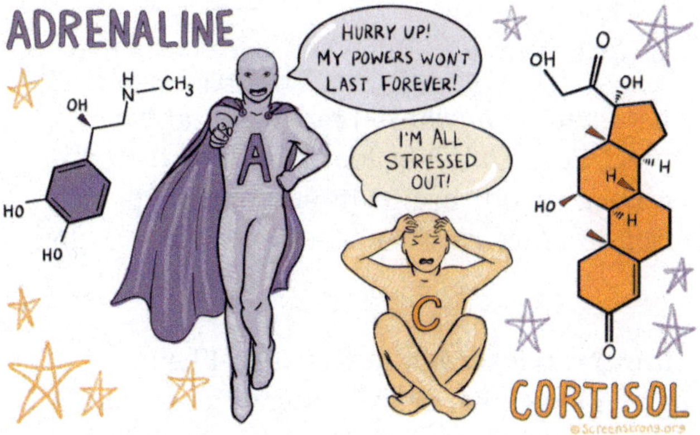

Adrenaline and **cortisol** are the two chemicals the brain releases when it perceives a threat. When released, the heart beats faster, blood pressure increases, and the body prepares to act quickly to escape danger.

Adrenaline gives us the short-term strength to fight the bad guy or run away from the bully. **Cortisol** triggers the increase of sugars (glucose) in the bloodstream for needed energy.

THE FIGHT-FLIGHT RESPONSE ITSELF IS STRESSFUL

If a bear was chasing you in the woods, you could run fast for a short period to get away because your adrenaline would give you a **boost of energy**.

However, this superpower would **not last forever**—only long enough for you to escape the bear. Then, your brain and body would need time to rest, recover, and return to normal.

BUT IT'S JUST A SCREEN, NOT A BEAR, RIGHT?

Our brains don't know the difference between being chased by an actual bear in the woods or being stressed on a screen. Both activities look the same to our brains and are equally stressful. This is because our brains interpret threats on a screen the same way they interpret real-life threats, even if we know the threats on a screen aren't real.

Scientists have discovered that many ***immersive screen activities***—like scrolling through social media, playing a video game, or watching videos—can also rev up the brain. These activities trigger the release of dopamine and stress hormones in our brains.

Can you believe it? **The brain reacts to danger seen on a screen the same way it responds to danger in real life.**

Let's look at some examples of threats that we may think are fun but are actually causing stress. Can you think of any more examples?

When we are on our screens, we may have fun, but so many little things can make us stressed that we don't even realize. Severe and prolonged stress from spending too much time on interactive screens can impair the brain's ability to function normally.

With prolonged screen activity, our brains don't have a chance to rest and recover. Since we all crave dopamine, we stay on our screens longer. As a result, our bodies may remain in a state of stress for an extended period of time.

"Chronic stress is also produced where there is a mismatch between fight-or-flight reactions and energy expenditure, as occurs with screen time; the physical energy needs to be discharged for the system to re-regulate. Once chronic stress sets in the brain, function suffers. "

—Dr. Victoria Dunckley, MD, author of *Reset Your Child's Brain: A Four-Week Plan to End Meltdowns, Raise Grades, and Boost Social Skills by Reversing the Effects of Electronic Screen-Time*

THE SCREEN STRESS PATHWAY

The stress pathway can be activated repeatedly when we are on our screens. It's like being on a rollercoaster every day—we might think it's fun, but our brains are flipping out!

The overproduction of stress hormones can cause us to be unable to focus on tasks. We can look like we have an attention disorder, even if we don't.

TOO MUCH STRESS MAKES US SHUT DOWN

The fight-flight system was never meant to be stimulated for a prolonged period. It is designed to be activated only in emergencies when our lives are genuinely in danger. Initially, a little bit of stress can seem exciting, but **our bodies can get compromised, exhausted, and even sick over time because of the repeated stress from screens.** This is because when the amygdala is overstimulated, anxiety outweighs the logical parts of the brain and causes panic. This is called chronic or toxic stress. **People with chronic stress are more prone to developing anxiety or depression.** Not only can it make us feel bad, but it can also make us stop feeling emotions altogether.

SUPPRESSED EMOTIONS

After the amygdala is overstressed and activates negative emotions like fear, anger, or frustration for an extended period, it will begin to shut down. This shutdown mode keeps the frontal cortex from performing its responsibilities for rational, reasoned responses.

Once the amygdala gets worn out, it can no longer do its job of warning us to stop doing the activity that's stressing us out. Therefore, we keep doing it, getting more and more stressed and even depressed. Sometimes, we start feeling nothing at all, making real life less enjoyable.

Some people turn to screens to escape because they think it's better to feel nothing than to feel bad.

Screen-based activities like social media, gaming, or binge-watching videos can temporarily distract from negative emotions. But in the long run, not feeling anything is worse for our mental health.

Understanding and accepting our good and bad feelings is essential to stay emotionally healthy.

SIX WAYS TO GET OFF THE STRESS ROLLERCOASTER

1

GOING OUTSIDE

Nature is a great way to reset our stress pathway.

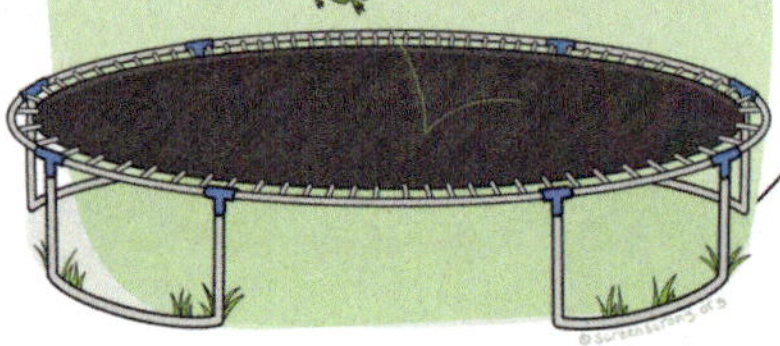

2

EXERCISING AND DEEP BREATHING

Activities that get us moving, like riding a bike or swimming, will relieve stress. Deep breathing exercises are another great way to de-stress.

3

JOURNALING

Writing down our feelings in a private place—not social media—is a great way to unload stress.

4

LEARNING A HARD SKILL

Challenging ourselves to learn something new and seeing the results (delayed gratification) causes us to gain confidence and feel joy over a job well done.

5

LISTENING TO MUSIC

Calm, relaxing music has always been a universal stress reducer.

6

GETTING TOGETHER WITH FRIENDS

Being together in the presence of friends has a way of dissolving a stressful day.

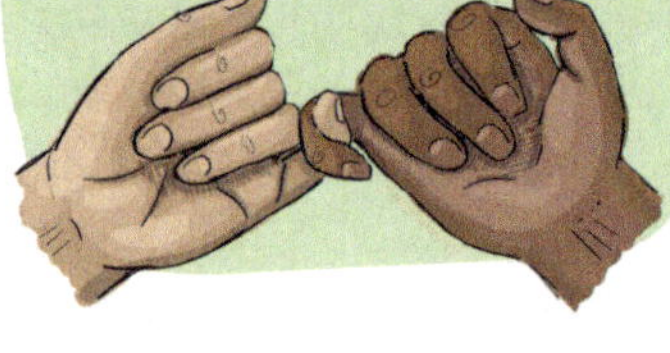

THE GOOD NEWS!

Thankfully, the brain can also remarkably recover from stress, especially when you are young. You can make changes now to have a healthy brain!

"Playing on our video games and phones for hours can hurt our brains and bodies. We need to get more exercise and be more CAT-hletic."

Skippy, The ScreenStrong Cat

How Can What I See Physically Affect My Brain?
Sight tells us more about the world than any other sense. The amount of information the visual cortex receives daily is so large that nearly half of the cortex is devoted to processing it. Everything we have ever seen in the natural and virtual world is embedded and saved in our incredible brains.

What happens in our brains when we see images?

1. The light from the image passes through the lens of our eye and hits the **retina**, which triggers chemical and electrical reactions that are then sent through the **optic nerve**.
2. The **optic nerve neurotransmitters** send messages to the visual cortex at the back of the brain to make you aware of what is on the image.
3. The information is then sent to other brain regions to be analyzed.

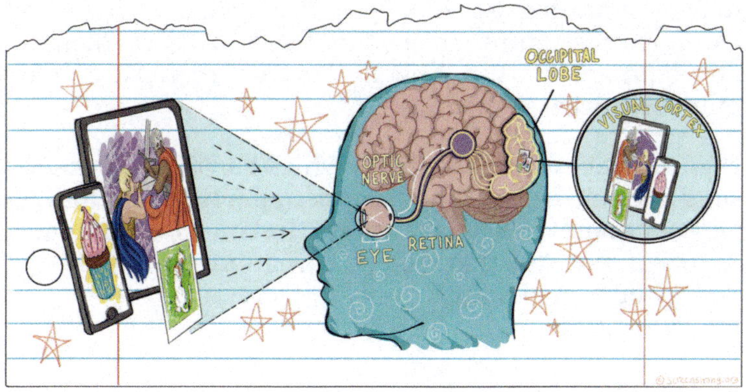

HOW SCREEN IMAGES PHYSICALLY AFFECT OUR EYES

Spending too many hours staring at a screen can cause eye problems. The light hits the retina directly when we see an image on a screen. Staring at direct light for long periods is hard on our eyes, so we tend to scan screens, and our eyes get tired. Too much screen time can affect vision, especially in children. Yikes!

Learn more about the impact screens can have on our eyes:

Excessive screen time strains the eye muscles, leading to fatigue and discomfort. The constant effort to focus, especially on bright or flickering screens, can **trigger headaches**, double vision, and difficulty concentrating.

Fast-moving images on screens force our eyes to constantly adjust and refocus, which can strain the eye muscles and lead to fatigue. Over time, this can cause **eye exhaustion**, discomfort, and difficulty focusing on other tasks.

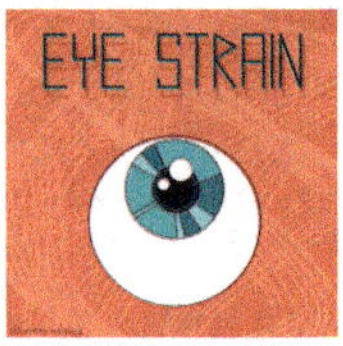

Sitting too close to a screen puts extra strain on the eyes. Too much close-up screen time can **weaken the eyes' ability to adjust** and focus on distant objects quickly.

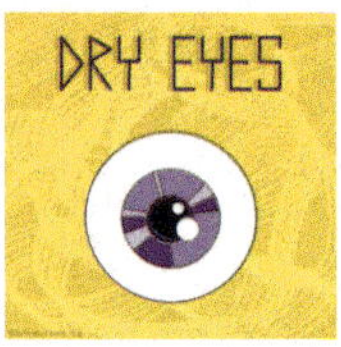

We tend to blink less when staring at a screen, which reduces the moisture on the surface of our eyes. Over time, **dry eyes can affect overall eye health,** making it harder to see clearly and even causing temporary blurry vision.

Staring at screens for long periods can lead to **nearsightedness**, making it harder to see far away. This happens because too much close-up screen time strains the eyes and affects their development. Studies show that more screen use and less time outdoors increase the risk.

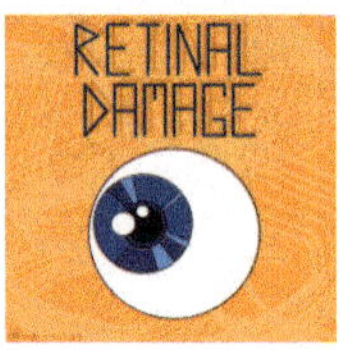

Digital devices emit blue light, which can damage the retina's light-sensitive cells, increasing the risk of **early vision loss and age-related macular degeneration.** The American Optometry Association warns that children are more vulnerable to this high-energy light than adults.

HOW TO PROTECT YOUR EYES FROM SCREEN OVEREXPOSURE

ADJUST LIGHTING
Make sure that your screen isn't brighter than the light surrounding it, or your eyes will get tired and have to work harder to see.

PRACTICE THE 20-20-20 RULE
Every 20 minutes, look at an object 20 feet away for 20 seconds. This allows your eyes to take a break and refocus. The American Optometric Association recommends the 20-20-20 rule.

KEEP EYES MOIST
Use artificial tears if needed to lubricate your eyes when they feel dry.

GO OUTSIDE EVERY DAY
Studies have shown children who spend more time indoors are more likely to develop nearsightedness, which means you can see up close but not far away. Rain or shine, go outside every day!

REDUCE GLARE
Screen glare can aggravate your eyes. Adjust the angle of your screen to avoid glare and see the content clearly.

EXERCISE EVERY DAY
Exercise at least 60 minutes every day. When possible, exercising outside in nature is even better. Getting plenty of natural daylight is essential for eyes to develop properly.

GET A YEARLY EYE EXAM
It is important to prevent eye problems by getting an eye exam once a year.

KEEP YOUR DISTANCE
Keep your screen about an arm's length or 25 inches away from your eyes. Your eyes work harder when the screen is too close.

USE BLUE LIGHT FILTERS
A blue light laptop filter will help reduce blue light and be easier on your eyes.

THE PHYSICAL EFFECTS OF GAMING

DOPAMINE SPIKE
Game play increases dopamine production. This sudden high dopamine increase can create cravings that lead to addiction, causing anxiety and depression when play stops.

AGGRESSION
Studies show that video game violence can lead to aggressive behaviors in real life.

CORTISOL
Increased cortisol production creates a stress state in the body which can lead to physical illness

VITAMIN D DEFICIENCY
Lack of sunshine creates a vitamin D deficiency. Over time, this can lead to weaker bones and other health problems.

FIGHT-OR-FLIGHT RESPONSE
The amygdala triggers the fight-or-flight alarm system in the brain when intensive play begins. Your body is not designed to stay in fight-or-flight for long periods of time; that is too stressful.

EYE PROBLEMS
Prolonged video game use leads to eye strain and dry eye from not blinking enough.

MORE PHYSICAL EFFECTS OF GAMING

FRONTAL CORTEX SHUTDOWN
The frontal cortex—the judgment center—begins to shut down after about 30 minutes of game play because the fight-flight center is taking over. There is decreased activity in this area dedicated to self-control and an increase in emotional arousal instead.

MUSCLE WEAKNESS
Muscles need testosterone to be strong. Testosterone is produced when you exercise and use your muscles. Gamers can develop weak muscle syndrome due to the lack of testosterone.

BLOOD SUGAR DECREASE
Gamers tend to crave sweet foods. Lack of exercise and increased junk food cravings can cause unhealthy weight gain.

ADRENALINE
Adrenaline, a stress hormone, is released in response to danger signals from the amygdala.

BLOOD PRESSURE INCREASE
Violent video game playing is associated with a significant increase in blood pressure when compared with watching TV or playing nonviolent games.

HEART RATE INCREASE
Gaming increases the stress response, which causes your heart to beat faster. It is unhealthy to have an increased heart rate due to stress for long periods.

CARPAL TUNNEL SYNDROME
Some gamers flap their arms to soothe the symptoms of carpal tunnel syndrome, which is caused by overusing their hands. Gamer's Thumb is also commonly caused by chronic soreness and overuse of hands.

POSTURE PROBLEMS
Gamers often sit with their shoulders rolled forward, their back hunched, and their chest caved in. This poor posture can cause shallow breathing, which can lead to anxiety and pain. Poor coordination is also a common side effect of too much gaming.

VIRTUAL VIOLENCE AND PHYSICAL AGGRESSION

Dr. Douglas Gentile is a researcher who studies the effects of video games and how game reward systems change behavior. He says that no child is immune to the lessons in aggression taught in a violent game. Spending a lot of time on games like *Fortnite* and *Call of Duty* could **desensitize us and change how we see the world**, making aggressive ways of thinking and feeling seem enjoyable.

Cartoon characters engaging in violent behavior have many of the same effects on the brain as viewing actual in-person violence. Your brain pays attention to cartoon characters and real life the same way, learning easily from both.

Aggression can take on these different behaviors in the real world:

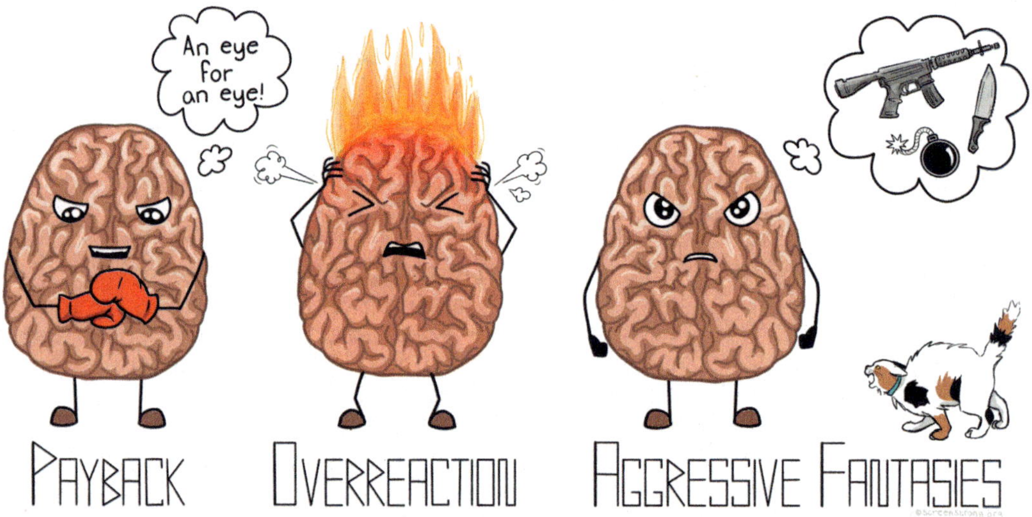

"If you hit me, then I hit you back."

Responding aggressively in the game is preferable and rewarded, so doing the same thing in real life starts to feel normal.

"Everyone is out to get me!"

Because of the time spent in the game, I assume people are trying to hurt me even if they do something by accident.

"I'd be really happy if he got hurt."

Spending time acting out aggressive fantasies in the game can make us start having aggressive fantasies about other people in our lives.

"Watching or playing a lot of violent media increases a person's risk for aggression, regardless of whether it is realistic or fantasy-themed. There are theoretical reasons to believe that fantasy violence (e.g., cartoons, violence against aliens, violence with unrealistic consequences) may actually be worse than realistic violence."
—Douglas Gentile, PhD, research scientist, educator, and author

The Physical Effects Of Smartphones

We are starting to see why gaming for hours can cause many physical problems. But what about time on smartphones?

Many smartphone problems are similar to those caused by gaming.

Let's learn some physical issues caused by smartphones.

PHYSICAL EFFECTS OF SMARTPHONES

TEXT NECK SYNDROME
Too much time spent looking down at a phone can strain neck muscles and cause tightness or spasms. Nerve pain can go to the back, shoulders, and arms.

HEADACHES
Too much screen time can bring on headaches. A combination of stress, muscle tension at the base of the skull, and eye strain is the usual cause.

NEARSIGHTEDNESS
Close-distance focusing can cause added eye strain and nearsightedness.

LACK OF VITAMIN D
When engaging on the phone, it isn't easy to spend time in the sun getting vitamin D, which is good for mental and physical health.

JUNK FOOD INCREASE
Junk food intake can increase by 25% for every hour of leisure screen time after one hour, according to the National Institutes of Health.

LACK OF EXERCISE
It is impossible to exercise while scrolling through social media. Childhood obesity is on the rise. We need to move!

DISTRACTED WALKING
Walking while distracted on a phone can cause injuries. Common injuries while using a smartphone include muscle and tendon strains, broken bones, and head injuries from falling down stairs or tripping while looking at a device.

INTERRUPTED SLEEP
Phone notifications can interrupt sleep. Spending more hours of the night on screens results in fewer hours of sleep. Stimulating content can also cause stress and decrease sleepiness.

CUBITAL TUNNEL SYNDROME
Cubital Tunnel Syndrome is caused when the user leans on elbows to text or bends them to hold the phone to the ear. This irritates the ulnar nerve. Symptoms include numbness and tingling in the ring fingers and soreness on the elbow or forearm.

DIGITAL EYE STRAIN
Tired eyes and fatigue from overuse can cause blurred vision. Viewing a digital screen for more than two hours can also cause pain and discomfort. Eyes can begin to burn and itch.

THUMB ARTHRITIS
Thumb arthritis causes pain and tenderness at the base of the thumb, where it meets the wrist. Pinching motions, like gripping a phone or texting with thumbs, are the types of movements that can cause pain or worsen the condition.

TRIGGER THUMB
When texting often, the thumb may get stuck in a bent position. When straightened, it may pop, which can hurt. This pop occurs because the sheath surrounding the thumb tendon can thicken, so the tendon can't slide freely.

DRIVING AND TEXTING
The phone should never be used when driving. It causes distractions and car wrecks. Thousands of people die each year in auto accidents caused by distracted driving due to phone use.

GERMS ON PHONE
Did you know that one in six phones has fecal matter on them because people take their phones to the bathroom with them? E. coli bacteria, which can cause fever, vomiting, and diarrhea, is also found on many phones. Gross!

BLUE LIGHT
Blue light from screens lowers the serotonin hormones that help induce sleep.

Do You Want To Be Stronger & Faster?

Regular physical activities make you feel better.

Scientific studies show that physical movement is critical to having a healthy body. Physical activity builds strong muscles and brains and also reduces symptoms of anxiety and depression. It even reduces the risk of obesity, diabetes, and cancer.

Outdoor activities add the bonus of sunshine, which is also critical for healthy development. **Spending more time in the natural world makes us stronger, faster, and healthier.**

One problem with screen overuse today is that we are becoming too **sedentary**, which means we sit too much and need to move more. It is hard to go outside and exercise once we get pulled into our video games and smartphones. Fortunately, the fix is easy and fun: trade screen time for physical hobbies, sports, and activities!

We become more physically active when we choose to go outside instead of playing video games and scrolling on smartphones. Here is a story about what happened to Ian when he traded his video game hours for playing basketball in the driveway.

Every day after school, Ian tossed his backpack on the floor, flopped down on the sofa, and turned on his tablet. He would game until his mom called him for dinner. Even then, he tried to keep playing, always asking for five more minutes.

One day, after repeatedly nagging him to set the table, his mom had had enough. After dinner, she hid his tablet in her closet and informed him it was time for a screen detox. Ian was furious! He refused to speak to his mother that night and was in a bad mood for days.

Finally, he realized that she wasn't giving in. After school one day, he grunted at his mom, grabbed his basketball, and headed outside to shoot some hoops. Day after day and week after week, his new after-school routine was to shoot baskets in his driveway. He started to enjoy it, and he got really good! Soon, other neighborhood kids joined him.

When basketball season came around, his best friend asked if he wanted to try out for the school team. "I don't think so," he replied. "I didn't make it last year." However, his best friend persisted. Ian finally agreed to try out, and guess what? He made the team! Making the trade—screen time for basketball time—paid off.

TRADE SCREEN TIME FOR MORE SPORTS

Without the temptation of screens to fill our downtime, **chances are higher that we will find ourselves spending more time outside.**

Chances are also higher that we will become better athletes. What are your goals for your mile time? How about your soccer, dance, swimming, or baseball aspirations?

Try something new, like mountain biking or tennis lessons. What team can you try out for? The options are endless. And the good news is that your body will be much healthier no matter how good you are. Plus, it's a lot more fun.

BENEFITS OF PHYSICAL ACTIVITIES

There are many physical benefits when screen time is not the focus of our day-to-day life. Remember, becoming ScreenStrong is not about removing all screens; it is about staying away from the screen activities that cause the biggest problems. Here are some physical benefits of being ScreenStrong:

Less time on screens means more time and motivation for sports. With practice, the body will get physically stronger and get better at sports!

Less screen time will lead to lower cortisol (stress hormone) levels, better heart health, and less stress and anxiety.

Less screen time leads to more physical activity during the day and fewer distractions at night. This can improve sleep.

Less screen time will give you more time for physical activities. This habit will lower the risk of obesity.

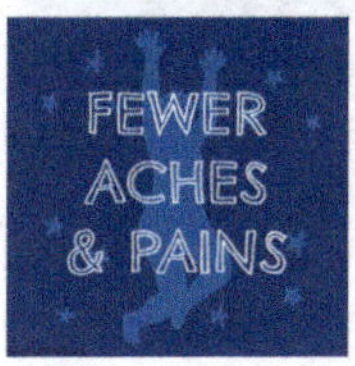

More physical activity leads to fewer body aches and a reduction in tech neck, joint pain, back problems, and other muscle issues often associated with too much sitting.

Less screen time will increase your chances of having better eye health.

SECTION 3
WHAT DOES SCREEN TIME HAVE TO DO WITH SLEEP?

"The average teen needs nine hours and 15 minutes of restful sleep each night for the brain to function at its best. That's a long CAT nap!"

Skippy, The ScreenStrong Cat

MORE SLEEP = BETTER BRAINS

Sleep is more important than you can guess. It is just as critical to our health as diet and exercise! The American Academy of Sleep Medicine recommends that teens (13-18) get between 8-10 hours of sleep every 24 hours; **some studies say 9 hours and 15 minutes.** Sleep is critical for teens. When adults don't get enough sleep, they become tired and drowsy, but the opposite can be true for kids; they can get **hyperactive, impulsive, stressed, and anxious.**

When we don't get enough sleep, our body sounds a stress alarm and prepares for an emergency. After all, it must be a real emergency to keep us up, right? But often, we lose sleep over staying up late to play a game or mindlessly scrolling on our phones.

Lack of sleep can lead to shorter attention spans and hyperactivity. It can affect our growth and our immune system, making us more susceptible to illnesses. lack of sleep can impact our ability to concentrate and learn and create other physical problems.

Poor sleep can lead to an increase in blood pressure and heart rate.

Poor sleep can cause cravings for fast food and sugar for quick energy increase.

Poor sleep can lead to more anxiety, less energy to control emotions, and less creativity.

WASHING AWAY STRESS!

Getting enough sleep is necessary for brain development, emotional well-being, and physical health. Did you know that during sleep, **cerebrospinal (suh-REE-bro-SPY-nal) fluid** washes in and out of the brain, helping to clear out waste and toxins? That's amazing.

Sleep helps us remember stuff.
While we sleep, our brains work hard to organize and reinforce the information we learn during the day. During sleep, all the knowledge from the day is transferred to the **long-term memory center** of the brain. Proper sleep improves focus, memory, motivation, emotional control, and, you guessed it, learning.

MORE SCREEN TIME = LESS SLEEP

Access to and using screens at bedtime is linked to poor sleep quality and excessive daytime sleepiness. Screen time does more harm than we might realize, as it significantly affects the quality of our sleep.

1. The **blue light from screens** alters our brains' sleep rhythms. Our brains see the screen light as daylight, causing a **shift in our bodies' sleep cycles**, and valuable sleep is lost.

2. Increased cortisol—the stress chemical released with screen overuse—**reduces melatonin**, the chemical that is needed to help us sleep.

3. Late-night surfing, streaming, watching risky content, and gaming consume more time than we realize. The ease of mindlessly scrolling on screens, especially when tired, makes it **easier to make bad choices at night when our defenses are the lowest.**

We think we are unwinding for the night by being on screens, but our brains are getting revved up, making it harder for us to go to sleep. Before long, we have been on our screens for two hours when we should be asleep.

LESS SLEEP = MORE PROBLEMS

Sleep-deprived teens have problems with attention, academics, risk-taking, stress-related disorders, and overall health. In addition, the level of cortisol rises, resulting in increased stress, anxiety, and **mood-related problems**. Read more below about the differences between teens who sleep well and those who don't.

DEPRESSED
When we are sleep deprived, we can be more anxious and apathetic because we don't have as much control over our emotions.

SLEEPIER
It is hard to stay awake during the day when we don't get enough sleep at night.

HEALTHIER
There is a greater chance that we will be healthier and happier when we're well-rested.

CLEARER MIND
We will have a sharper mind when we get enough sleep every night.

LOWER MOTIVATION
It is harder to do anything productive when we are constantly tired leaving us less satisfied and moody.

POOR TIME MANAGEMENT
Getting up in the morning is more challenging when we're tired, and we may need help being on time and getting homework done.

LOWER GRADES
When we stay up late, focusing the following day on tests and classwork is harder, resulting in lower grades.

BETTER GRADES
Chances are higher that our grades will improve with enough sleep because our memory will improve.

BETTER AT SPORTS
With enough sleep, we are more focused and better at sports than when we don't get enough sleep.

DRAW A LINE TO MATCH THE HEALTH OUTCOMES OF SLEEP-DEPRIVED KIDS AND THOSE WHO ARE WELL-RESTED

KIDS WHO ARE SLEEP-DEPRIVED

KIDS WHO ARE WELL-RESTED

Have good memory function

Get lower grades

Are calmer

Are more likely to be obese

Are able to focus

Are more motivated

Get better grades

Have mood-related problems

Are better able to regulate emotions

Can be forgetful

Get stressed easily

Take more risks

"Do you want to do better in school, perform better in sports, have more focus during the day, and feel physically better? Then get more sleep, you need NINE HOURS A NIGHT."

—Dr. Adriana Stacey, MD, psychiatrist

SLEEP AND SPORTS

Sleep improves motor function, muscle recovery, focus, and motivation when you play sports. It also enhances memory and learning. Sleep reduces stress hormones and improves overall performance. Coaches love it when their teams get enough sleep!

IMPROVES REACTION TIME

FEWER MENTAL ERRORS

REDUCED INJURY RATE

Sleep is the brain's #1 rest and recovery tool. It is critical for letting go of the stresses of the day. If we want to prevent the harmful effects of chronic stress and excel in sports, school, and life in general, we must get a good night's sleep!

CAN YOU REMEMBER?

1. The American Optometric Association recommends the 20/20/20 rule. What is this?
   - ☐ Every 20 hours, start a new video game so you don't get tired of the old one.
   - ☐ Every 20 minutes, text your friend so they don't feel lonely.
   - ☐ Every 20 seconds, "like" a post so you will build your social media following.
   - ☐ Every 20 minutes, look at an object 20 feet away for 20 seconds.

2. What is the fight-flight response? Check all that apply.
   - ☐ The body's reaction to stress
   - ☐ What birds do in the winter
   - ☐ What happens when you fight with your brother
   - ☐ What happens when you play a video game

3. How much sleep does a teenager need every night?
   - ☐ Six hours
   - ☐ Seven hours and 25 minutes
   - ☐ Nine hours and 15 minutes
   - ☐ Eight hours

WHAT CAN YOU DO RIGHT NOW?

- ☐ Get one hour of exercise every day.
  What can you do to move more? ______________________________
- ☐ Follow the 20-20-20 Rule: every 20 minutes, look at an object 20 feet away for 20 seconds.
- ☐ Get outside every day after school before dinner instead of getting on a screen.
- ☐ Stay away from violent video games and violent content on social media.
- ☐ Avoid blue light at night an hour before bedtime.
- ☐ Avoid arousing screen activities in the evening one hour before bedtime.
- ☐ Get a non-smartphone alarm clock.
- ☐ Don't sleep in your bedroom with a phone, computer, TV, or other technology.

NOTES

CHAPTER FOUR

MENTAL:
YOU'LL HAVE A SHARPER BRAIN

CHAPTER 4: INTRODUCTION
MENTAL: YOU'LL HAVE A SHARPER BRAIN

Welcome to Chapter Four.

Great job on the last chapter! Understanding how screens affect our bodies is key.

Being ScreenStrong doesn't mean being anti-screen or screen-free. It's about using screens as tools and for occasional entertainment—like watching movies with friends—while avoiding addictive activities like video gaming and social media.

This chapter explores how screens can distract us and hurt our ability to think and learn. While technology offers benefits in the classroom—like instant access to information and collaboration—it also brings challenges and risks that can outweigh these benefits.

You'll learn to distinguish educational screen use from entertainment and explore how multitasking and screen distractions affect attention. Behind every amazing person is a brilliant brain, just like yours, but research shows that the distraction of handheld screens can limit your brain's potential, especially in the classroom.

In this chapter, watch for answers to:

1. *How many thinking tasks can your brain do at once?*
2. *Do smartphones in the classroom help or hurt learning?*
3. *What happens when we handwrite notes instead of typing them?*

Let's dive in!

Lydia

"Research reveals that some educational screen time is good for learning, but smartphones in the classroom? FUR-get about it. MEOW!"

Skippy, The ScreenStrong Cat

When it comes to learning, how do we tell the difference between screen activities that will help us and those that will hurt us?

One way to tell is that truly **educational technology** does not stimulate the production of high levels of dopamine that **entertainment screens** do. Are we craving more essays to write or Excel sheets to build? Probably not. Educational screen activities are generally easy to walk away from; entertainment screens, on the other hand, are not. This is a huge difference. Let's try to keep this in mind throughout the chapter.

BIG PROBLEMS COME IN SMALL PACKAGES

In the days before compact tablets and smartphones, the desktop computer was the go-to device for many people. These computers were large, clunky, and impractical to carry in backpacks or pockets. Although users of desktop computers were susceptible to the lure of addictive screen activities just like they would be on any other device, they didn't spend as much time engaging in these activities because the desktop computers weren't portable.

LET'S SEE HOW SCREENS HAVE CHANGED OVER THE YEARS.

TOO BIG TO PUT IN A POCKET
The larger format of old screens kept people from taking them everywhere, so they were less likely to overuse them.

SLOWER
Old technology was slow. The slower it was, the less addictive it was. It was boring to wait for programs to load.

PORTABLE SIZE; FITS IN BACKPACK
Laptops are easy to carry to private places in the house. Easy access is a universal trigger for every addiction.

FASTER SPEED
Instant feedback leads to overuse.

EASY TO HIDE
Because of their small portable size, screens are easier to hide from parents and teachers.

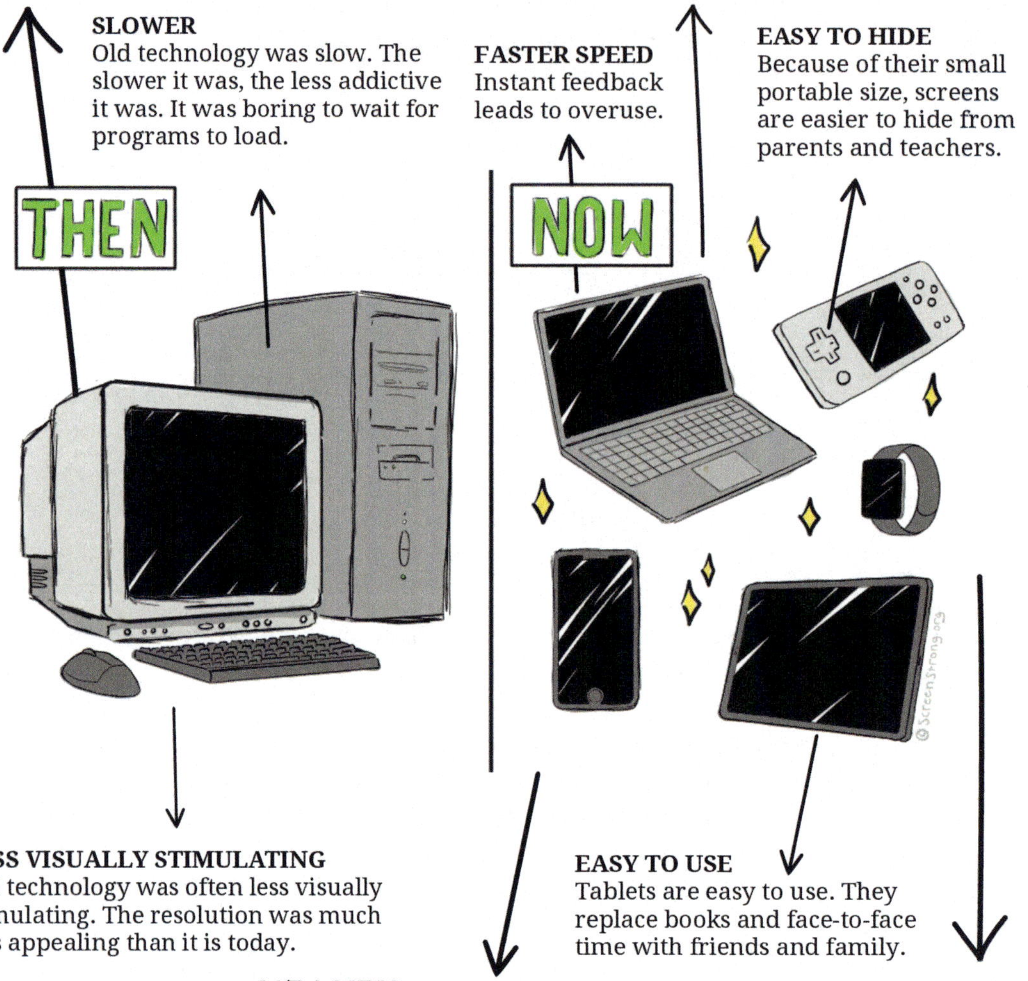

LESS VISUALLY STIMULATING
Old technology was often less visually stimulating. The resolution was much less appealing than it is today.

EASY TO USE
Tablets are easy to use. They replace books and face-to-face time with friends and family.

24/7 ACCESS
It's unnecessary and unhealthy to have a little computer in our pockets all day.

WITH YOU ALL THE TIME
A smartwatch is distracting because you are wearing it. It interrupts your concentration all day long.

The portable nature of smaller screens makes them easy to access, which is a critical factor in addiction. **The risk of overuse is higher with smaller screens.**

It is easy to see how having addictive handheld screens available during the school day causes problems. These devices constantly demand our attention, acting as significant distractions that can negatively impact learning. Now we know. The big problem with screens in school has to do with one word: **attention.**

How Long Can We Pay Attention?

Now that our brains are used to such fast-paced content and entertainment, we crave attention-grabbing media every few seconds. The result? It doesn't take very long for us to get bored—less than eight seconds. Media companies are working hard to dazzle us and grab our attention before we get bored. They have to cram enough interesting content into those eight seconds if they want to keep us watching.

Our brains are being **rewired to prefer fast-paced screen content over the pace of real life,** and we lose the most essential skill for school: attention—the ability to concentrate and focus on something without being distracted. The more developed our brains are, and the more we practice executive functioning skills, the better we are at paying attention.

Imagine, for a moment, that you are a goldfish. Would you get bored after swimming in the same little bowl your whole life? Probably not.

By the time a goldfish swims to one side of the bowl, it has already forgotten what's on the other side.

Goldfish have a nine-second attention span because they have tiny brains. Our brains are much bigger, allowing us to pay attention for much longer periods of time, but only if we are not distracted.

Did you know?
Watching TikTok videos for 20 minutes leads to a decline in attention span and working memory. The brain becomes accustomed to short bursts of content and can no longer handle deep learning tasks that demand longer focus. Too much fast-paced screen content harms brain development, resulting in a lower attention span and increased anxiety and depression in young users.

SCREEN DISTRACTIONS HURT LEARNING

When schools allow smartphones in the classroom, grades go down. Learning is challenging when smartphones are present because comprehension requires uninterrupted attention, time, and focus.

Interruptions. Checking text messages during class causes a loss of time in two ways: the time it takes to read the text and the time it takes to refocus on the topic the teacher is covering after we read the text. This task-switching interrupts focus and reduces class performance, causing us to learn at a slower pace.

Loss of focus. Eventually, these distractions will chip away at the brain's ability to maintain focus. The attention span will shorten. This hurts the ability to think deeply for extended periods, which is critical for learning.

Don't allow distracting screens to make learning harder than it needs to be.

"The digital world is a toxic environment for kids' brains. Rather than making super learners, it has stunted their mental growth."

—Joe Clement and Matt Miles, coauthors of *Screen Schooled: Two Veteran Teachers Expose How Technology Overuse Is Making Our Kids Dumber*

When too much time is spent gaming, watching videos, or using social media, **brains get used to fast-paced excitement**. This makes it harder to focus on things like listening to teachers, reading textbooks, or writing essays. School activities may become boring because there is a craving for a more stimulating environment than the classroom offers. Students can disengage from learning. When students dream about gaming, always reach for phones in class, or fidget to stay focused, it's a sign that their brains may be growing dependent on screens.

<u>Question</u>: Why is having handheld devices at school a big concern?
<u>Answer</u>: **Multitasking**.

Handheld screens are crafted to capture and keep attention, creating a constant battle in the brains over where the focus should be. In the school setting, the primary focus for students should be **learning** and **building relationships**, but small devices like smartphones easily distract students from these tasks.

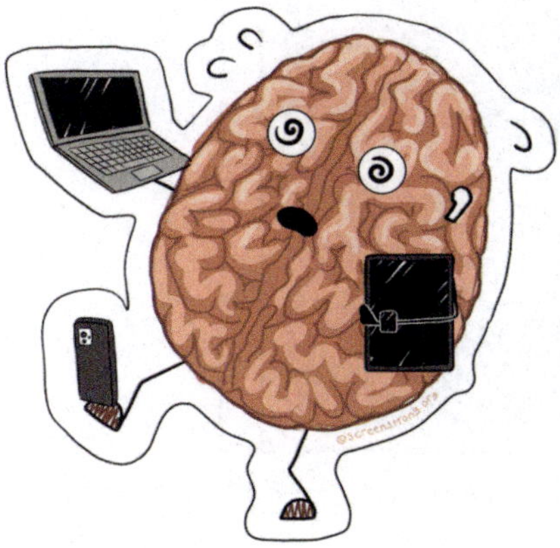

CAN WE MULTITASK?

Our brains can only concentrate on one task at a time, regardless of how smart we are. We can learn to shift quickly between tasks but only **focus on one "thinking" task at a time**. It would be more accurate to call this "speed-shifting" or "task-switching."

A nonschool example of this is watching TV while trying to read a book at the same time; the brain can't do it. The same is true when we are in class. We can't pay attention to our screens and to the teacher at the same time.

MULTITASKING IS A MYTH.
Most people think they can multitask, but studies show it is impossible. No matter how good we think we are at doing multiple things simultaneously, we are not very good. It's impossible to think about two things at once. **The result of multitasking: an overworked brain that is too tired to learn.**

MULTITASKING
LEADS TO LOWER GRADES

Rapidly switching between tasks—like checking email and social media during class—harms attention by:

1. Reducing the ability to **focus**—less time for deep thinking and performance
2. Increasing the number of **mistakes made**—errors sneak in
3. Reducing **creativity**—little energy for new ideas
4. Reducing **memory retention**—long-term memory is reduced

The cost of multitasking is high.
Regaining focus and getting back on track after being interrupted can take longer than you think; some studies say up to 25 minutes.

Research shows that students who have a phone nearby—or sit behind other students with a phone out—get lower scores on average than distraction-free students. Many schools don't allow smartphones because of the **distractions** they cause. Some college professors don't allow laptops during lectures because students can't resist online distractions when they have them out.

LEARN MORE ABOUT SCREEN DISTRACTIONS IN SCHOOL

Can you think of any more that we didn't mention?

At the end of the day, learning is hard. Don't allow distracting screens to make it even harder!

Now that we've seen an overview of the problems of screen distractions, especially in school, let's zoom in on another big problem with having small screens in the classroom: **cheating**.

Smartphones Don't Belong In Schools

"During my sixth-grade year, I was **highly addicted** to YouTube. I watched thousands of YouTube videos during my school day and essentially skipped that entire year of school.

I was shown a video of XXX pornography on a kid's personal cell phone at the lunch table. This same student, because of Discord and other social media platforms, was influenced by the trend of saying, *Just kill yourself.* This student repeatedly told me I should kill myself daily. This led to suicidal ideations. I was lucky I told my mom and asked for help but not everyone is able to do that. She found ScreenStrong. I no longer have these extreme ideations. With the help of certain teachers and my parents using KBS to teach me about screens, I have had many positive changes in my life. I cannot say the same for some of my peers I see each day.

Phone-free schools are awesome. Kids need a place to be kids and socially interact with each other again.

—Colin, ScreenStrong Teen

FOSTERING HEALTHY PHONE-FREE HABITS IN SCHOOL

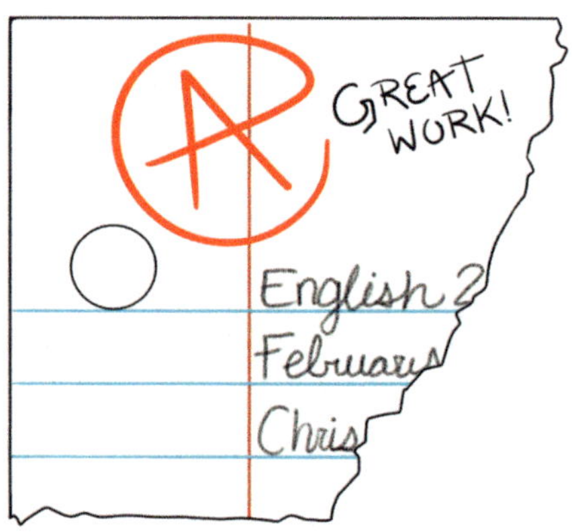

- Trade your smartphone for a basic phone
- Leave your phone at home
- Take notes on paper
- Sit in the front of the class
- Try out for the school play & a sports team
- Go outside every chance you get
- Make more friends
- Make plans for screen-free weekends
- Take the 7-Day Digital Detox Challenge

BENEFITS OF PHONE-FREE SCHOOLS

Benefit One

Boost Your Focus, Boost Your Grades!

- More attention to learning
- More engagement with teachers
- Better grades

Benefit Two

Build Stronger Friendships!

- More time for social interaction
- More practice reading social cues
- More relationships built

Benefit Three

A Stress-Free School Day!

- Less anxiety throughout the day
- Fewer opportunities for online bullying
- More happiness and calm

Benefit Four

Move More, Feel Better!

- More active breaks during the school day
- More interest in extracurricular activities
- More motivation for sports

SECTION 2
IS CHEATING ALWAYS WRONG?

> "Cheating is so tempting when you have a smartphone in class. Leave your phones at home so you don't have a cheating CAT-astrophe. Don't be a cheetah!"
>
> *Skippy, The ScreenStrong Cat*

Cheating is defined as acting dishonestly or unfairly to gain an advantage. Screen access at schools opens the door to the temptation to cheat during school. **Unlimited access to information on our screens makes cheating hard to resist.** When we have a smartwatch, smartphone, or laptop nearby, the temptation to cheat can be overwhelming.

Many students don't even believe that cheating is wrong. However, the truth about cheating will never change. It's always wrong, and it will always hurt us. Ask your teacher if you're unsure if something is considered cheating or if it is just a shortcut to help you learn.

Check out the next page for some common examples of cheating.

ELEVEN COMMON EXAMPLES OF CHEATING

1. Googling an answer during a test is CHEATING.

2. Secretly using your phone in class to get answers you've saved on it is CHEATING.

3. Copying homework assignments or essays is CHEATING.

4. Taking a photo of a test and giving it to someone else is CHEATING.

5. Asking Alexa for an answer is CHEATING.

6. Using Chat GPT is CHEATING.

7. Using Photo Math or another Math app to solve a problem is CHEATING.

8. Getting on a VPN to access another server at school is CHEATING.

9. Answering a friend's question in a text while taking a test is CHEATING.

10. Purchasing essays and term papers from online services is CHEATING.

11. Going around parental controls or a school firewall is CHEATING.

Reasons For Cheating

The first step to breaking a cheating habit is to understand **why** you are cheating.
Below are a few reasons why students cheat:

For The Thrill Of It

Sometimes kids cheat because they see it as a competition or a fun challenge to conquer.

Out Of Fear

Sometimes kids cheat because they fear hard work or getting a bad grade.

For A Friend

Some kids help friends cheat because they want to be accepted or they feel sorry for their friend.

Cheating Hurts

1 **Cheating hurts one's ability to learn.** Learning builds on previous knowledge. Cheating causes essential steps in the learning process to be skipped.

2 **Cheating hurts social integrity.** When students cheat, they lose the trust and respect of close friends, peers, and teachers.

3 **Cheating hurts the future.** Cheating is a dead end. It will hurt in the long run more than it will help now. It can even become part of a permanent academic record and decrease the chances of college entrance or a future job. That is serious.

Can't Stop Cheating?

Cheating is a bad habit, like any other habit. Make a goal and a plan, and never cheat. Here are some ideas on how to reduce the chances of cheating:

As with any bad habit, access is the problem. Don't use a smartphone at school or for homework.

Create a support network. Ask teachers for homework help to raise grades. Being honest with parents really helps.

Join a study group with friends. Setting up a reward system when goals are reached can be very motivating.

Are Your Friends Cheating?

Most kids find it hard to stand up to cheaters because it takes a strong leader to stand up for what is right. But cheating can ruin a friendship. The first thing to do when you see friends cheating is to talk with them about it and get it out in the open. Tell them you saw them cheat. Hiding it will only make it worse. After that, encourage them to tell the teacher and ask for help. Sometimes, it is easy to fall into the cheating habit when our friends are cheating, so be careful not to join in.

Here are some more tips. Can you think of others?

TALK WITH YOUR FRIEND

In private, ask your friends why they are cheating. Be empathetic but honest, and tell them it isn't right. Without judgment, help your friends understand that they are hurting their future.

STUDY WITH YOUR FRIEND

Studying together is more fun and can help your friend learn the material.

ASK A TEACHER FOR HELP

Suggest that your friends talk to a teacher; offer to go with them to make it easier.

"FUR-get about typing notes when you can get smarter by writing them on paper!
BTW, what is smarter than a talking cat? A spelling bee!"

Skippy, The ScreenStrong Cat

Best Practices For School

Cognitive or thinking tasks, like homework, require significant effort. Concentrating on one thing at a time takes a lot of work. **Focusing on using your whole brain without screen distractions is the best way to learn faster and more.** There is no way around it; learning can be lonely, but it will go by quickly if you are efficient. A good rule is to find a quiet place to study and separate study time from leisure time. More will be accomplished. Study hard, then play hard!

SHORTEN YOUR HOMEWORK TIME

©screenstrong.org

ONE THING AT A TIME

When we use multiple devices at the same time during homework, we get distracted. Our brains get overwhelmed. This wastes time and decreases the ability to remember what we've learned. Homework can seem to take forever.

TIP: *Remove all extra screens when you do homework. Don't even text your friends. Once you finish your online assignments, shut the laptop to prevent other distractions while continuing to study.*

TIP: *Choose the same place to study every day. This routine will help you remember more!*

Does Background Music Help?

Do you like listening to music when you do your homework? Most people do. But have you ever wondered if it hurts you more than it helps?

Research suggests that some music can improve your mood and help you relax, but **not all study music is created equal**. Music with lyrics activates the language-processing centers of your brain. This means that if you are trying to read new content while listening to the words of a song, your **comprehension will worsen,** and you will get distracted.

Listening to some types of music is not only distracting but is also considered multitasking.

What music may help with homework?

Music with no lyrics is best. Classical music, for example, has no lyrics and is typically calm. Also, it is mostly unfamiliar, so it can better serve as background music. Avoiding recognizable tunes works well when studying.

***TIP**: Find a "reading music" playlist that is calm and soothing for you. Make sure it's ad-free, and keep the volume low.*

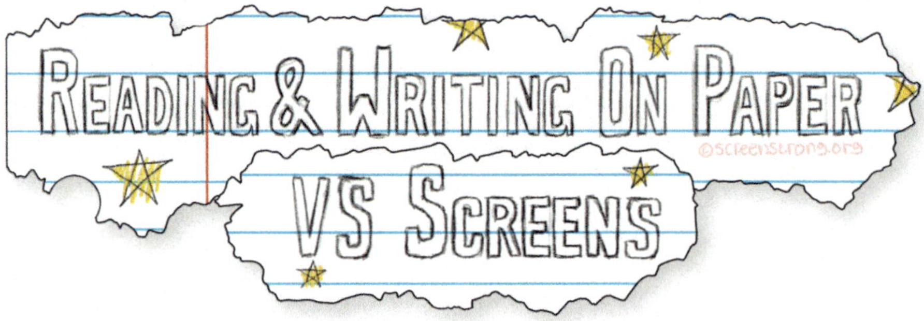

WANT TO LEARN FASTER? CHOOSE A BOOK!

One thing proven to help us learn better is using a physical book instead of reading online. Reading a book stimulates more senses and is less distracting than reading the same content on a screen.

SENSE OF TOUCH
The physical activity of touching the book and the pages helps to keep us alert, more focused, and engaged in the content.

NO (FLASHY) DISTRACTIONS
Avoiding distractions like pop-ups, ads, flashing bright colors, or inappropriate internet content helps us stay on task.

EASIER ON THE EYES
Reading a book is easier on our eyes because the light is reflected off the page rather than directly into the retina. That is why we tend to scan a screen but read a book. Books are better for concentrating and recalling content from memory.

SENSE OF SMELL
Even our sense of smell helps us engage in the learning experience. A book is more likely to trigger a memory than a screen because each book has a unique smell.

LOCATION OF CONTENT ON THE PAGE
Seeing the location of the content on the page helps us recall information more easily. We lose that reference point when scrolling a screen.

THE ACT OF TURNING THE PAGES
When we turn the pages, we get a sense of order and timing, where we are in the story. This helps with comprehension. Doing this also gives us a sense of accomplishment as we make it through the book.

"Children and teens intuitively know what is best for their health and learning, which is why they prefer teachers, books, paper, and pencils over screens in school settings."

—Cris Rowan BScOT, BScBi, SIPT, author of *Virtual Child: The Terrifying Truth about What Technology Is Doing to Children*

WRITING ON PAPER VS. TYPING IS BEST FOR LEARNING

Taking notes by hand engages more areas of the brain, resulting in better memory. When we type, we're more focused on getting every word exactly as it is. When we handwrite, we summarize and organize the content in our heads first, then transfer it to paper. This allows for deeper learning. Often, we customize notes to fit our learning styles and personalities, making them more effective. This process helps us **understand and remember** content better.

REVIEW the three benefits of choosing to write notes by hand vs. typing them:

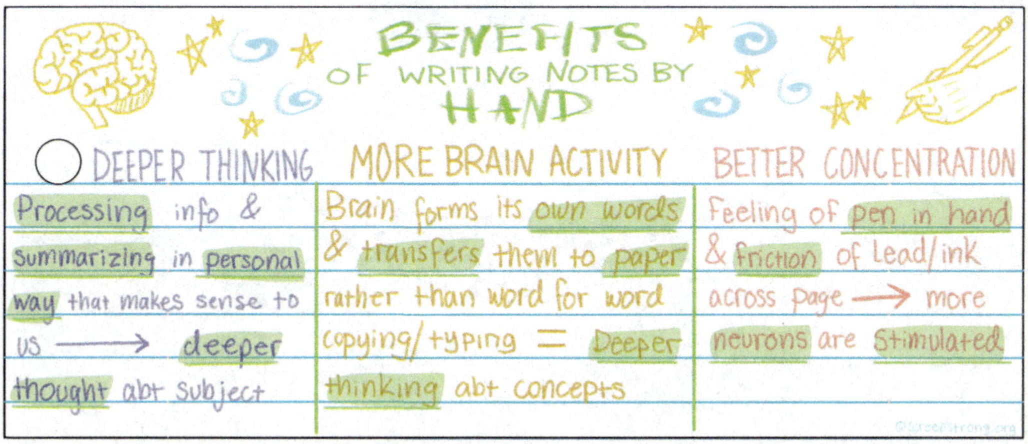

Choosing to be ScreenStrong means focusing more on activities in the natural world than the virtual world. Sure, we need to use screens for some school and homework, but when we learn to move our entertainment time offline, we will be more likely to get better grades; plus, we'll have more fun, be less stressed, and be healthier overall.

MORE LEARNING BENEFITS OF BEING SCREENSTRONG

You will be **more calm and less anxious** without screen distractions.

Investing time with people learning new things will make you **more well-rounded and interesting.**

You will have more time to form **meaningful relationships** with peers and teachers.

You will be more **productive with homework** without temptations to play video games or scroll.

You will love reading when screen activities do not distract you, and you can discover the new wonderful world of books.

You will spend more time **exploring extracurricular activities** like sports, music, drama, and art when screens aren't filling your days.

SCREEN TIPS... FOR SCHOOL AND BEYOND!

These tips aren't meant to hold you back but are intended to expand your life. Don't be afraid to share your goals with others. You have everything it takes to succeed in school and life and to have good friends. Take the lead, and be the first to do the right thing. ScreenStrong has your back!

USE YOUR SCREEN AS A TOOL, NOT A TOY
Screens are for research and learning, not for entertainment when you are in school.

YOUR SCREENS DON'T BELONG TO YOU
They belong to your parents.

USE A TEXTBOOK BEFORE A SCREEN
Paper beats screens every time.

DON'T TAKE A SMARTPHONE TO SCHOOL
Undistracted class time pays dividends for the rest of your life; you will meet more people.

LUNCHTIME IS FOR SOCIALIZING, NOT SMARTPHONES
Sit with people who are not on their phones.

TAKE NOTES ON PAPER
Handwriting instead of typing notes increases focus, makes you smarter, and gives you an academic advantage.

MAKE YOUR BED EVERY MORNING
One daily success will lead to many more.

FIND A GOOD BOOK SERIES
Reading for pleasure at age 15 is an indicator of future academic success. What novel are you reading now?

SIT IN THE FRONT OF THE CLASS
Kids who sit in the front of the class get better grades. They also cheat less.

DON'T CHEAT
No grade is worth the shame and regret of cheating—you will be sorry you did.

GET MORE SLEEP THAN YOU THINK YOU NEED
Sleep will lower your anxiety. Teenages need nine hours of sleep every night!

DON'T HACK SECURITY SETTINGS AT SCHOOL OR HOME
Security filters keep you safe. If you are fascinated with hacking skills, take a computer class to learn ethical hacking skills.

TRY OUT FOR THE SCHOOL PLAY OR A SPORTS TEAM
Your school years are a great time to do this.

DON'T FALL INTO THE VIDEO GAME VORTEX
Don't even start playing. It's a waste of time and you may not get out.

GO OUTSIDE EVERY CHANCE YOU GET
It is hard to be anxious in nature.

EMBRACE YOUR BASIC PHONE THROUGH HIGH SCHOOL
Hug your parents for getting it for you.

CAN YOU REMEMBER?

1. How many thinking tasks can your brain do at once?

- [ ] One thousand
- [ ] Twenty-four
- [ ] One
- [ ] Six

2. Smartphones in the classroom make it easier to cheat.

- [ ] True
- [ ] False

3. What happens when we handwrite notes at school?

- [ ] We stimulate more neurons in our brains.
- [ ] Our brains remember what we are writing better.
- [ ] We think about the letters by forming them in our heads.
- [ ] All of the above

WHAT CAN YOU DO RIGHT NOW?

- [ ] Never have a phone out during homework. By focusing on your homework, you will get it done SO much faster and have more time to do your hobbies and hang out with friends.

- [ ] Choose physical books over screens for reading. Ask your parents for your own public library card if you don't have one yet.

- [ ] Sit at the front of the class; this will help you make eye contact with your teacher and focus better.

- [ ] Take notes on paper, not on a screen. If you do this, you will get better grades because you will remember more. Try it before your next test.

- [ ] Ask your parents if you can sell the gaming console and use the money to take a trip to your favorite sports, music, or clothing store.

CHAPTER FIVE

SOCIAL: YOU'LL HAVE DEEPER FRIENDSHIPS

CHAPTER 5: INTRODUCTION
SOCIAL: YOU'LL HAVE DEEPER FRIENDSHIPS

Welcome to Chapter Five.

This chapter is all about something that makes life better: friendship.

Strong social connections aren't just fun—they're essential for our growth and health. But spending too much time on entertainment screens like social media or gaming can actually make us feel lonelier. Why? Because online interactions can't replace real, face-to-face connections, where meaningful conversations and shared experiences happen.

In this chapter, you'll learn why in-person friendships are stronger than virtual ones and how focusing on real-life connections can reduce stress, anxiety, and even depression. Building friendships takes practice, but with the right strategies, you'll create bonds that last a lifetime.

Here's what to look out for in this chapter:

1. *How long does it take to turn a casual acquaintance into a good friend?*
2. *What's the secret ingredient for making your friendships stronger?*
3. *What three skills can you practice to become more empathetic?*
4. *Why are parents better guides than friends?*

Friendships are one of life's greatest adventures—let's dive in!

Adam

"It's true, the more time you spend online the less time you have to make good FUR-iends!"

Skippy, The ScreenStrong Cat

BENEFITS OF FRIENDSHIPS

Did you know that socializing with others is essential to our health? When we socialize with others in person—as opposed to virtually—our brains are stimulated in different and fulfilling ways. Being together with friends causes our brains to release healthy doses of dopamine, which not only makes us happy but also relieves stress at the same time. In general, relationships that are built on in-person interactions are much stronger and better for you.

"Spending time with friends in person is way cooler than hanging out on a screen with them. Growing up, my friends and I rode our longboards around the neighborhood, played basketball in the driveway, and stayed up late playing fun board games. We even named our group and made T-shirts. I would have missed out on all our adventures if I had stayed locked in my room all day playing video games or scrolling on my phone. I wouldn't trade all those memories for a phone or video game. After all, you can't go fishing with someone on a screen."

—Evan, a ScreenStrong Teen through high school

HERE ARE A FEW MORE REASONS HAVING FRIENDS IS GOOD FOR US

SHARPENING COGNITIVE THINKING SKILLS
Socializing sharpens memory and cognitive skills. It's true! Hanging out with our friends makes us smarter.

LIVING A LONGER LIFE
Research says that socializing in person makes us healthier and helps us live longer!

FEELING HAPPIER
Participating in a social group will increase our sense of overall satisfaction in life.

FEELING LESS LONELY
We will be less lonely when socializing with friends in person rather than online.

GROWING IN INDEPENDENCE
Friend groups provide us with opportunities to practice our social problem-solving skills. We become more independent and mature as we grow confident in this ability.

FEELING A GREATER SENSE OF BELONGING
Friends help us connect and belong to the community outside our immediate family unit. Being accepted into a social group is an important part of healthy teen development.

LEARNING MORE SOCIAL SKILLS
Besides our families, friendships are where we learn social skills and empathy. Learning how to relate to others starts with a small group of friends.

The Magic Number

How Many Friends Should I Have?

Did you know that our brains are like social muscles? They can only manage a limited number of relationships before they get exhausted. Scientists have discovered that our **inner circle**—the people we are closest to—**is limited to about five.** This includes a few very close friends and, of course, our family. The people in this group are the ones we love and trust; we know we can depend on them in a crisis.

The next level in our social circle consists of about **15 people** we consider **close friends,** significant but not as close as our inner circle.

Beyond these two levels are people we're **casually** acquainted with, somewhat familiar with, or barely know. We interact with them occasionally, but the bond isn't as strong as with our inner circle.

Our close and casual friends may shift in and out of our inner circle as we grow and our lives change.

What a relief! **We don't need to be best friends with everyone, and we don't need to keep up with 100 friends on social media.**

Relationships require time.

Researchers say it takes **over 200 hours** to transform an **acquaintance**, or someone we hardly know, into a **close friend.** This time consists of sharing experiences and making memories together in person.

Every hour we spend on screens is time we could have used to build strong relationships in person. While it may seem like we're making friends on our screens, scientific findings suggest that screen relationships lack the personal and genuine depth found in face-to-face interactions.

The word "**shallow**" means superficial or lacking depth. It is a great word to describe why relationships formed in the virtual world can be less fulfilling.

Screen communication promotes surface-level conversations. It is a convenient tool for quick check-ins, managing get-togethers, and sending invites. However, **it doesn't allow for the face-to-face interactions** and shared experiences needed to build meaningful connections and deepen relationships with your closest friends and family.

BROKEN PROMISES

Before social media, the average teen hung out in person with friends almost every day after school. Then, they had conversations with each other every night on landline phones. They were more confident in their social skills because they had so much practice, and data suggests they were more willing to go out on dates.

Believe it or not, research shows that teens who did not have access to smartphones and social media were happier than teens today. This is mainly because they spent their social time in person, building a bank of experiences and memories. On the other hand, teens today spend most of their time on smartphones and social media—on average, nine hours every day.

Studies show that the amount of time teens spent face-to-face together dropped after 2009 when smartphones became available. The irony is that while screen culture has made big promises—claiming that social media is a great way to make friends and be more social—we feel more left out and lonely than ever.

Our desperate attempts at online friendships are failing.

"During middle school and high school, I had a basic phone—text and talk only. That meant my attention wasn't glued to my phone, endlessly scrolling, which gave me a certain freedom. So I got together with friends for coffee or to hang out, face to face. I think it helped me, particularly now that I am a resident assistant in a dorm, and my job includes meeting with students in person to get to know them on a deeper level."

—Aubrey, ScreenStrong college student

One day, a college-age boy was driving on the highway at night when his car broke down. Over the next hour, he posted on social media that he was stranded and needed help. To his dismay, **no one even responded.** He knew his friends were on their phones as they always were, but no one reached out to help him. His conclusion: **"My generation has no real friends."**

Even if we think we have a lot of online friends, we may still feel very lonely because casual friendships cannot fill our inner circle. We may not have anyone we can rely on when we need help or feel like we have close friends who really know us.

True friends experience life's ups and downs together and support each other. And if our car breaks down on the side of the road, leaving us stranded, real friends will come to the rescue!

Our friends need us, and we need them.

We have learned that human connections flourish when we engage in shared interests and activities in person. The strongest bonds are forged in the natural, physical world. However, it is not just about being together. Building tight bonds and cultivating genuine friendships takes **time** and **commitment**. The more time you put in, the more rewarding the benefits.

What can you do to nurture your friendships today?

SECTION 2
OH NO! WHAT'S MISSING ON MY SCREEN?

> "The only way to truly know how someone feels is to see for yourself, LITTERly. Our friends deserve genuine CAT-nections with us."
>
> *Skippy, The ScreenStrong Cat*

Have you ever been misunderstood in a text?
Have you ever been hurt by a friend or stranger on social media?

You are not alone. Screens offer many conveniences and practical tools to make our lives easier, but there is a big gap. Unfortunately, the most significant gap in the digital world centers around our biggest need: **human connection.** This gap exists because two of the most critical pieces of communication that help us fully understand people are missing online: **eye contact** and **social cues**.

Eye contact is the act of looking directly into one another's eyes. It is a critical communication skill and can be harder than it seems.

Social cues are communication signals that don't involve words and are challenging to notice on a screen, even during a video chat.

FACES TELL ALL

Faceless communication, like texting, is less trustworthy and less efficient. When we can't see someone's face, it takes longer to understand what is really being said, and it can't satisfy our social needs. A voice or video call is better than a text, but most of our social time online is spent texting, posting, and commenting. That's why screen time is a weak method for building friendships and meeting social needs.

Emotional Intelligence (otherwise known as emotional quotient or EQ) is the ability to **manage both your own emotions and understand the emotions of people around you**. Self-awareness, empathy, and social skills are a big part of EQ. If we're honest, most of our time online is spent in isolation as we scroll, watch, and post. We are not developing a strong EQ when we are on a screen.

The more we learn to read feelings in person, the deeper our relationships will be. And, as a bonus, we will feel much less lonely. Face to face is a win-win!

"Having a high EQ (emotional intelligence) is twice as important for life success as having a high IQ. And the only way to develop a strong EQ is through lots and lots of face-to-face interaction."

—Tom Kersting, psychotherapist and author of *Disconnected: How to Protect Your Kids from the Harmful Effects of Device Dependency*

LOW SOCIAL METER SCORE
As much as online communication tries to meet our social needs, it will never meet those needs 100%. That's why depending mostly on online communication can make us frustrated and depressed.

EYE CONTACT
Our eyes show our emotions through expression. Are they filled with tears? Are they wide open? Are they looking away? Making eye contact is necessary for deep understanding.

THE AMYGDALA
The amygdala helps us interpret and understand our friends' emotions. Is our friend trustworthy or dangerous?

DOPAMINE
Being face to face stimulates our brains to trigger healthy amounts of dopamine. This is why we feel good when we are in the presence of our friends.

MIRROR NEURONS
These are neurons that light up when we see our friends. They help us recognize the emotions of others and determine if the person is happy or sad.

FUSIFORM GYRUS
This part of the brain is dedicated to reading the emotions on someone's face. This act is so critical to survival that this area of the brain is dedicated to recognizing facial cues.

THE BENEFITS OF FACE TO FACE

Our brains are wired to read emotions best by seeing human faces. When we can't see our friends' faces, make eye contact, or read nonverbal cues, we don't always know how our friends feel. We may have to guess. It is difficult to tell if someone is hurt or in pain without being in their physical presence and seeing their facial expressions.

More face-to-face interactions will help us **learn and understand the emotions of the people** around us, which is necessary for friendship building. Time with friends together helps us in the following ways.

MORE LOVE

People feel special and important when we choose to spend time together with them in person. Making your friendship a priority is a necessary part of building good friendships.

MORE EMPATHY

Spending quality time with friends can help us become more empathetic and caring. It is hard to develop empathy with people we can't see face to face.

MORE HAPPY MEMORIES

We remember the time with friends in person more than in the virtual world because more of our senses are engaged. Creating memories with others builds a strong foundation for our friendships. Memories hold our relationships together and make them special.

Companies invest a lot of money and resources to try to fix the problems of faceless communication. The emoji was invented to do just that. While these virtual emotions may be cute, **emojis are not enough** to replace experiences with natural human emotional reactions. Just like many other shiny promises in the virtual world, these virtual emotions are empty. They will never be as good as the real thing!

The only way to truly know how someone feels is to see for yourself, literally. Our friends deserve genuine connections with us, not a substitute or second best. Don't you think your friendships are worth more than a smiley face emoji?

Social cues are **nonverbal signals** that people use when they are communicating. They help show thoughts, feelings, and intentions. These signals can be simple or exaggerated but often **convey more information than words alone.** In addition, these cues add deeper meaning to conversations. They fill in gaps to complete what is communicated, giving everyone the whole picture. Here are some examples of social cues.

THE ABILITY TO READ SOCIAL CUES IS MISSING ONLINE

Without this essential conversational element, we have less information about what our friends say and feel, which can weaken our relationships over time.

THE END RESULT?

- Feelings of being left out and alone
- Miscommunication and hurt feelings
- Broken friendships and increased isolation

We are not born with the ability to read social cues. We must practice by spending time interacting with our friends. Just like practicing the fundamentals of sports, practicing the fundamentals of personal communication is essential.

BUILD YOUR FRIENDSHIPS ON SOLID GROUND

Becoming a master of **eye contact** and **reading social cues** will set us up for solid and deep friendships. These strong friendships, built on face-to-face time, will help us through the storms of life. Spend more time nurturing friendships!

"Don't be a sour puss. You will go far in life when you learn to be a more empathetic PURR-son!"

Skippy, The ScreenStrong Cat

Deep down, we all want to be known and loved for who we really are. Our brains know how important this is, so it has special neurons—**mirror neurons**—that allow us to feel what others are feeling and be in tune with their emotions. These neurons are activated when we are in the presence of others; they help us experience empathy.

Empathy is the ability to share someone else's feelings or experiences by imagining what it would be like to be in their shoes. Along with the desire to be loved and accepted, we have a strong need for others to share in our feelings of happiness and pain. We need friends to show empathy to us; likewise, our friends need us to show empathy to them. It's a huge part of being a good friend!

"Understanding others is essential to being a good human, especially a caring friend. Giving and receiving empathy creates closer relationships while screens can push you farther apart. Spend time connecting with your friends instead of only connecting over a screen."

—Annalise, a ScreenStrong Teen through high school

LEARNING EMPATHY SKILLS

When you practice the following three skills, you will be better at empathy.

RECOGNIZING FEELINGS

A fantastic way to cultivate empathy is by practicing social skills. Paying attention to our friends by spending time with them and trying to understand their feelings shows them that we genuinely care about them.

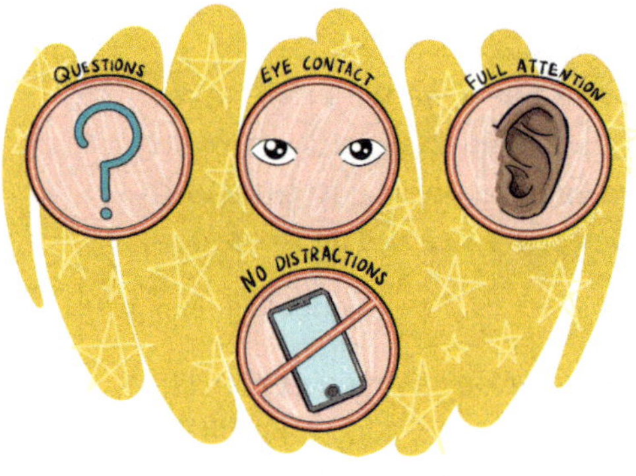

LISTENING WELL

Listening well includes using multiple senses: asking questions, making eye contact, and focusing your full attention on your friend. It is impossible to listen well when you are also looking at your phone.

SHOWING YOU UNDERSTAND

Show your friends you care by repeating back to them what you think they are feeling. This validates them and makes them feel loved because you are showing them you are really listening. Here's an example: *"I hear you saying that your feelings are hurt because I told you I would call, and I forgot. I totally understand because I would feel the same way."*

HOW TO USE SOCIAL CUES TO SHOW EMPATHY

Imagine your dog passed away. Would you rather have your friends send you a text or pause what they're doing to come over to your house and be with you? Most likely, you would want them to be with you in person.

NOT SPEAKING
Sometimes, saying nothing—just listening—while a friend expresses feelings speaks louder than anything that could be said.

EYE CONTACT
Looking people in the eyes is one of the strongest ways to show we care for them. People who struggle to maintain eye contact are seen as less empathetic and trustworthy.

BODY LANGUAGE
Turning toward your friend, uncrossing your arms, and nodding as you listen all help your friend know you care.

PHYSICAL PRESENCE
Nothing can beat the act of going out of your way to be physically present with a hurting friend. Taking your time to care is a strong empathetic quality.

PHYSICAL TOUCH
Human touch can send emotional signals. We can convey empathy through touch as effectively as we can with facial cues.

TONE AND VOLUME OF VOICE
Using a soft voice communicates understanding. Words matter, but tone can be even more critical.

FACIAL EXPRESSIONS
Facial expressions that convey compassion include a relaxed face, furrowing in the center of the brow, eyelids not raised, and head and body oriented forward. Being with a friend in person to see facial expressions is crucial when showing empathy.

We can practice empathy by being kind to our pets. Pets can convey empathy, too!

WHAT TO SAY TO SHOW MORE EMPATHY

Sometimes, it's challenging to think compassionately about our friends because we are naturally more focused on ourselves and our needs than theirs. Below are some phrases we can use to show empathy to our friends. These statements help people feel **understood, loved, and supported**. Practice them often!

SUPPORTED

"I'm on your side."

LOVED

"I wish you didn't have to go through that."

UNDERSTOOD

"I think I understand how you feel."

UNDERSTOOD

"You're making total sense."

LOVED

"That sounds frustrating."

SUPPORTED

"That must have annoyed you."

SUPPORTED

"I think I hurt your feelings. Can we talk about it?"

LOVED

"How can I help you with this?"

UNDERSTOOD

"You're having a rough day. I get it."

HOW TO GET BETTER AT EMPATHY: PRACTICE

We can't get better at basketball by simply watching basketball; we must be in the game to improve. The same is true with practicing empathy.

The only way to know how our friends really feel is by **getting off our screens and into the game of life with them.** The natural experiences we share together in the physical world will help us become empathy experts.

MORE EMPATHY MEANS MORE FRIENDS

Building relationships goes beyond playing video games together or gathering followers on social media. It demands devoting our time, being **actively present**, **understanding** our friends, and **demonstrating genuine care.** Mastering the art of empathy leads to deeper friendships and a greater sense of being loved.

The rewards of showing empathy benefit everyone involved!

"Being empathetic is more important than intelligence. Learning how to feel what your friends feel leads to more friends and contributes to your future success."

—Dr. Adriana Stacey, MD, psychiatrist

"I'm TAIL-ing you—parents are the best life coaches you will ever have. Don't let your screen be your guide!"

Skippy, The ScreenStrong Cat

YOUR FAMILY IS YOUR HOME BASE

One of our most important tasks during our teen years is learning how to be social and make good friends. However, **friends should never replace the role of parents and caring adults in our lives.**

Strong bonds with our families keep us centered and prevent us from being easily swayed by negative cultural influences. Having strong relationships with our families also makes us happier.

PARENTS & TRUSTED ADULTS ARE OUR BEST LIFE COACHES!

Imagine your favorite sports team. You have favorite players on that team, right? Those players didn't reach the big leagues alone or just by listening to their friends. They achieved success because they had excellent coaching throughout their sport's journey.

Our friends are like our teammates, and our parents, teachers, and other caring adults are like our coaches. They all serve critical roles but very different positions.

Parents and peers serve different roles.

Our parents and trusted adults—including our extended family—serve as our life coaches and most loyal advocates. **Their love is unconditional**, and they offer wisdom and guidance. They always have our backs!

While our friends are super important, they play different roles in our lives. They love us but cannot provide the same level of guidance needed for our lives. **They can never replace the unique role of our parents and trusted adults.**

HOW PARENTS HELP

Our parents—and trusted adults—are more concerned about our safety and well-being than anyone else, including our friends and even ourselves. They look ahead and **protect us from harmful cultural influences**. Helping us stay on track, they nurture our talents and come alongside us as we strive to reach our potential. **They protect our best interests in ways that no one else can.**

In other words, when we are growing up, **our parents' job is not to be our best friend but to be our coach, anchor, and compass**. Sometimes, we might not agree with them or their rules, but we have to trust that they know what's best for us and that they love us more than our friends.

Our values are the principles that affect the decisions we make and how we live. Our families, not the digital world, serve as our best guides in shaping our values.

Our families play a crucial role in helping us discover what makes us unique. They are well-equipped to assist us in discovering our life purpose.

Our families are invested in safeguarding us from the potential risks associated with cultural influences, a role our friends cannot fulfill.

"When I was really into my social media, I felt like it became my family. It was a terrible feeling to be disconnected from my real family. I am so glad my parents rescued me before it was too late."
—ScreenStrong Teen

CHOOSE FRIENDS WISELY

The drive to copy our peers is strong. We all subconsciously need to be like the people around us, fit into the peer group, and be accepted. This drive is a built-in survival skill because there is strength in numbers, and it's especially strong during our teen years.

We hear many voices when we are on social media and in gaming communities. The online world has many overwhelming choices. **But these choices are not filtered by people who care about us**, like our parents or other trusted adults. As a result, too many voices can cause confusion, leading to anxiety and depression. Friends must be chosen carefully because friends influence our values.

Too Many Influences

It is easy to let peers and **influencers** on social media play a significant role in shaping how we act. For example, they can affect what we like, how we dress, and even how we think about ourselves. We can forget who we really are.

Online influencers don't have our best interests in mind like our parents do. That's not their job. Often, their job is to gain popularity so they can make money from their audience, us. Sure, they're entertaining, but they aren't a good source for shaping our personalities and values.

PARENT ORIENTED VS. PEER ORIENTED

Research shows that teens who **stay well-connected with their families** and trust their parents have an easier time in all areas of life. When teens rely on peers to be their guides, they **expose themselves to more problems** from negative cultural influences.

DRAW A LINE TO CONNECT THE STATEMENT WITH THE CORRECT CHOICE BELOW:

WHEN PARENTS OR TRUSTED ADULTS ARE GUIDES

WHEN PEERS ARE GUIDES

- BETTER SELF-CONTROL
- MORE INCLINED TO TAKE DANGEROUS RISKS
- BETTER EMOTIONAL REGULATION
- MORE LIKELY TO USE DRUGS AND/OR ALCOHOL
- HIGHER SELF-ESTEEM
- LESS ATTACHMENT TO SIBLINGS AND FAMILY
- LESS PROTECTION FROM CULTURAL INFLUENCES
- LESS LIKELY TO USE DRUGS AND ALCOHOL
- BETTER GRADES IN SCHOOL
- MORE INSECURE
- LESS LIKELY TO MAKE BAD DECISIONS
- LOWER SELF-ESTEEM
- LESS LIKELY TO BE STRESSED AND ANXIOUS

CAN YOU REMEMBER?

1. How long does it take to turn a casual acquaintance into a good friend?

- ☐ 115 Snaps
- ☐ Playing *Fortnite* with them for 25 hours in total
- ☐ 200 in-person hours spent together
- ☐ Receiving a minimum of 19 TikTok videos from one person

2. What is the most important element of communication that will help deepen your friendships?

- ☐ Eye contact
- ☐ Facial expressions
- ☐ Tone of voice
- ☐ All of the above

3. What skills can you practice to help you improve your empathy?

- ☐ Recognizing feelings
- ☐ Listening well
- ☐ Showing you understand
- ☐ All of the above

WHAT CAN YOU DO NOW?

- ☐ Write the names of three good friends you would like to spend more time with in person. ______________, ________________________, ___________________________
- ☐ Plan to meet up in person with friends at least once a week. Start having non-tech social gatherings at your home.
- ☐ Plan a sandlot baseball game or organize a few friends to meet for a hike, bike ride, or get-together without screens. Having experiences together offline is the first step to building true friends.
- ☐ Join a club or sports team to meet more people and expand your potential friend group.
- ☐ Delete social media.
- ☐ Ask your parents for a basic talk/text phone (with no internet access or apps) so you can use it as a planning tool but not for social time. Go to ScreenStrong.org to get ideas.

NOTES

CHAPTER SIX

EMOTIONAL: YOU'LL BE LESS ANXIOUS

CHAPTER 6: INTRODUCTION
EMOTIONAL: YOU'LL BE LESS ANXIOUS

Welcome to Chapter Six.

In today's world, some kids and teens believe that spending time on screens will make them happier, but new studies show the opposite. Certain things we see on screens can affect our emotions and make us feel worse.

Screen time contributes to persistent worry, sadness, frustration, and increased impulsive behavior. This explains why kids, teens, and even adults who use screens too much are less happy and often feel lonely.

In this chapter, we will learn how screens affect our emotions and moods and how we can choose the pathway that gives us the greatest chance of being emotionally healthy.

In this chapter, look out for the answers to the following questions:

1. *What is online social rejection?*
2. *What are some emotional benefits of being ScreenStrong?*
3. *What happens when we are more confident?*

Let's go!

Lydia

> "Our feelings are affected by the things we see on our screens. FUR real!"
>
> *Skippy, The ScreenStrong Cat*

WHAT WE SEE AFFECTS OUR MOODS

Let's kick off this chapter with a review to refresh our understanding of how our brains work.

Way back in Chapter Two, we learned how our bodies react to situations by releasing hormones called **neurotransmitters**. These chemical messengers control everything from how our bodies function to our moods and emotions. **Stress hormones** like adrenaline and cortisol help manage stressful situations by increasing heart rate, blood pressure, and blood sugar levels. On the other hand, **feel-good hormones** like dopamine and oxytocin create feelings of well-being, happiness, and excitement.

These chemicals control our moods. For example, when we have positive thoughts, the stress hormone cortisol decreases, and the brain produces serotonin, fostering a sense of well-being. Normal serotonin levels contribute to happiness, calmness, reduced anxiety, improved focus, better sleep, and emotional stability.

OXYTOCIN | ENDORPHINS | CORTISOL

Let's see which hormones are released when you view the following images.

OXYTOCIN

The hormone oxytocin is released when we see our pet or best friend. Oxytocin fosters feelings of connection and love.

ENDORPHINS

Endorphins are released when we see a picture of a tasty treat, making us feel good—and hungry!

CORTISOL

When we see violence, even in the form of cartoon violence, our brains release cortisol and can easily go into the fight-flight mode, which causes stress.

NEGATIVITY BIAS

When we are on screens, our attention is often drawn to topics that make us sad or stressed. This can affect our moods.

That's right. As odd as it may seem, our brains are fascinated by negative, extreme, and outrageous things. Scientists call this tendency the **negativity bias.** This impulse causes us to spend too much time looking at scary content or content that makes us angry, even when we don't mean to.

As discussed in Chapter Two, complex algorithms and programming decide what shows up on our feeds. This means we see a lot of negative media. Negative content can affect how we feel and think.

WHAT WE SEE AFFECTS OUR ACTIONS

The content we view on our screens significantly impacts our brains. It alters how we perceive the world, shapes our beliefs, and influences our behavior. This is due to the natural tendency to compare ourselves to others, imitate how others act, and believe what we see—whether it's accurate or not.

"Before we get online, our life looks pretty good. After we spend time online, we compare ourselves to what we see, most of which is not how things look in real life. Many things people post are different from the truth. We feel more worried and can even feel sad when we constantly compare ourselves to their fake lives."

—Dr. Adriana Stacey, MD, psychiatrist

COMPARING OURSELVES TO OTHERS

We all have a tendency to compare ourselves to the looks and actions of others. You could say that being a copycat is part of human nature!

It's no different with screens. We can't help but **automatically compare** ourselves to what we see online. However, so much of what's online has been altered or filtered, so we are comparing ourselves to impossible standards.

As a result, we get jealous. **We aren't satisfied with how we are,** which makes us sad and anxious. We wish that we could look more like what we see online. We learn that it is really true: **"Comparison is the thief of joy."**

IMITATING OTHERS' BEHAVIOR

Media content is such a powerful influence that it can prompt us to change our behavior to match what we see. It can trick us into thinking we have a problem that we don't actually have. This is called a **perceived flaw.**

This perceived flaw can then drive changes in our behavior, often in extreme ways, as we attempt to address what we perceive as an issue. **We might replicate the actions and behaviors of people online in an attempt to "fix" ourselves when we were fine to begin with.**

For example, images can convince us that our body type is not good enough, tricking us into thinking that we are overweight when we are not. **And no one likes being tricked.**

BELIEVING WHAT WE SEE

Deception occurs when **our brains automatically trust what our eyes perceive, even when it is false**. We often click on content that captures our attention through sensational headlines, clickbait, and false promises. Our curiosity can expose us to numerous falsehoods, leading to deception.

Many online influencers and movements aim to help us believe their messages and join their ranks without question. **They skillfully package their messages to lure us in.**

The more exposure we have, **the more confused we may become.** There is no worse feeling than finding out that we've been scammed, taken advantage of, or lied to.

REJECTION HURTS

It is certainly possible for us to benefit from the nice things people say about us on social media. However, let's be honest. **The things we remember the most are the negative things.** And there are a lot of them.

Some of the negative things we face online can be direct (like specific criticism) or indirect (like being purposefully left out of the group). When we talk about the **negative side of our online experiences, it can be summed up in one word: rejection.**

Rejection is harmful to people of all ages, but data shows us that the **pain from rejection is felt the deepest during the teen years.** This is unfortunate since most teens are on social media—a place where they will be rejected often. In fact, it is common for teens to feel more rejected online than in real life. This is partly because it feels like there is no escape online.

Once we are part of the online world, it can feel more important than reality and often begins to feel like our real world.

CYBERBULLYING

Another form of rejection commonly found on screens is **online aggression,** also called **cyberbullying**. This involves using words, pictures, and videos to harm, intimidate, or coerce another person.

To see why online aggression is so common, let's look at it from a bully's perspective.

1. **Bullies love attention.** Online bullying is an effective way of hurting someone's feelings because **everyone else online can see it,** making it very public.

2. **Bullies like to hide behind a screen.** Cyberbullying is easy to do because the nature of screens makes it highly **impersonal and private.** Because bullies can hide behind a username and a screen, they feel less guilt for the harm caused by their words. It is much easier to be mean to someone when we aren't face to face with them.

3. **Bullies seek the easiest way out.** Cyberbullying is something that **all people can do.** Even if certain people would never bully someone in real life, they can easily bully someone online in major and minor ways. Hiding behind an anonymous username allows a non-bully to become a real bully in the virtual world easily.

The fact that cyberbullying is **both public and private at the same time** makes it **incredibly easy to be more damaging.**

WORDS USED TO HURT

Another way our screens have power over us is through our own words or those of our friends or followers. The phrases below the graphic show examples of online acronyms and phrases that can be used to hurt others.

Let's see some examples of what online rejection can look like.

"You don't belong here."

"You should have used a filter."

"You are UGLY!"

"Did you see what Maddy wore today? Horrible."

"DIRL"—Die in real life

"KYS!"—Kill Yourself

"You are such a simp."

PHUBBING

Have you ever felt hurt because your friends were more focused on their phones than on you, even when you were together in the same room?

Phubbing is the bad habit of **ignoring or snubbing the person physically present** with you to look at your phone instead. It often stems from the constant urge to check our phones every few minutes. Phubbing is a **form of rejection**, and it can make anyone feel terrible, possibly even sad. When this happens, it is best to take the lead, suggesting a new activity and a change of environment, like going outside if possible.

WHEN TO SEEK HELP

No one should have to experience rejection or bullying alone.

We need to pay close attention to how our feelings and emotions change when we are online. If we feel hurt, we need to **reach out to our parents or another trusted adult for assistance.** If our friends are also facing challenges, we should encourage them to do the same.

DISCUSSION QUESTIONS

Discuss these questions with a parent or trusted adult.

How did that make you feel? What did you do about it?

How did that make you feel? Have you ever purposely not tagged someone in a photo?

Did you tell anyone about it? Most people don't—but you definitely should! Tell your parents, a teacher, or a trusted adult. No one should face this alone.

How to experience less rejection

By choosing to live without social media, we can avoid online rejection. While no one can guarantee a rejection-free life—especially during the teen years—eliminating toxic screens for now makes us less likely to suffer from unnecessary, painful experiences. That is the goal. Experiencing rejection pain doesn't help make us immune to it. We will be better equipped to deal with the effects of rejection when we are older.

> "Are you FELINE sad? Try getting off your screen and going outside more. Outside is my favorite place!"
>
> *Skippy, The ScreenStrong Cat*

THE MENTAL HEALTH STORM- DON'T GET SWEPT AWAY!

Mental health problems impact our thoughts, emotions, and self-perception, often resulting in changes in our behavior. When we make our screen world our primary community and the focal point of our life experiences, it's easy to develop mental health problems, including anxiety, depression, and isolation from family.

Relying too heavily on screens can contribute to decreased confidence in our social skills and even confusion about identity.

HOW DO MENTAL HEALTH PROBLEMS DEVELOP AS A RESULT OF TOO MUCH SCREEN TIME?

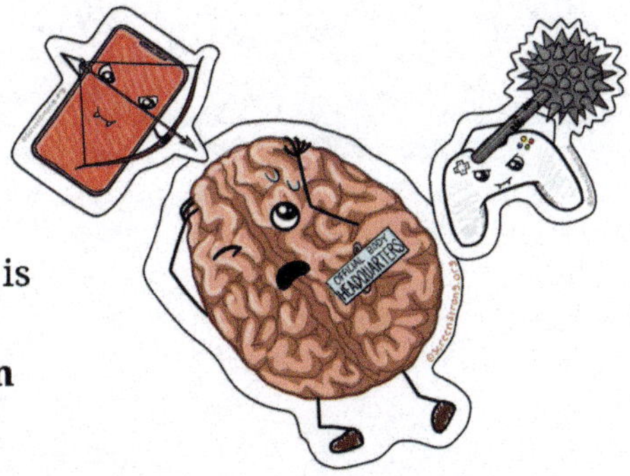

The science behind mental health problems is complicated, but to put it simply, these problems are **symptoms of a stressed brain that has lost its balance.**

Think of our brains as the headquarters of our bodies. Too much time spent on certain screen activities is like an **attack on the body's headquarters.** Mental health problems are the result of the damage done by these attacks.

HOW CAN I TELL IF I HAVE A MENTAL HEALTH PROBLEM?

Have you ever lost your appetite or couldn't sleep if something upsetting happened at school? That is an example of how physical changes are signs of a stressed brain. Our physical bodies react to our emotions, giving us clues that something is out of balance. Some symptoms of imbalances include:

Poor sleep and appetite changes can mean you are worried and can be signs of a stressed brain.

Irritability and rapid or dramatic shifts in emotions, commonly called mood swings, are warning signs of mental health imbalances.

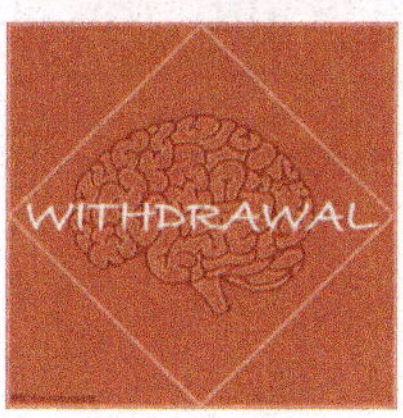

You may withdraw as you lose interest in activities you previously enjoyed.

Armor

Just like we have physical needs—food, water, exercise—we have psychological needs, too. These basic psychological needs fall into three general categories:

1. The need to belong: **Live in Community**
2. The need to learn and master skills: **Build up Competence**
3. The need to act independently: **Grow in Confidence**

The right balance of community, competence, and confidence can act as armor for our brains, helping to keep us emotionally stable and strong. If the brain's armor is weak or missing altogether, our mental health is at greater risk.

Some screen-based interactions are fun and convenient, but they do not help build the suit of armor that our emotional brains need to stay healthy and strong. Realistically, **psychological needs will not be fully met in the virtual world.**

When we discover how to get these basic psychological needs met offline, we are more likely to have a strong suit of armor protecting our mental health from attacks.

Building a strong foundation for mental health begins with where you belong: **Your community.**

The importance of our larger community is second only to the significance of family connections, which was covered in Chapter Five. Humans are meant to be social, so we **crave meaningful relationships in larger communities.**

Our need to be social is as strong as our need for food and water. Gaining a sense of purpose and meaning by connecting with a larger group of people who share our values is a critical developmental task for teens and adults.

Your family. Your family (or guardian) is your first community. They are part of your inner circle. Stay connected to them and enjoy the support and direction a strong family foundation provides.

Your faith community. This is an example of a larger community with shared common values. A spiritual community provides a natural environment where we can experience hope and support. This community encourages us to exercise gratitude and service toward others. These are essential ingredients for the development of healthy emotions and fulfillment.

Scientific research shows that belonging to a religious community helps us cope better with stressful life circumstances and gives us meaning, hope, and support through all life stages. These are all necessary for good mental health.

Competence is the knowledge and ability to do a skill well. Some examples of these skills for teens include communication and social skills, general life skills, and academic skills.

Our mental health gets stronger with increased competence. As we gain more general life skills, we become more well-rounded, more calm, and less anxious. Feeling a greater sense of control and purpose is essential for our emotional health. When we are free from the anxiety and confusion that can be created by depending on the virtual world too much, we will have more bandwidth to expand our skills and for our personalities to flourish.

The more we practice building new skills, the more equipped we are and the less stressed we will be when we learn new things. We will also be more equipped not to panic when things go wrong. **Our competence grows every time we learn and practice new skills.** Competence is indeed the gift that keeps giving!

How do we gain more competencies? We build our skills by carving out more offline time in our schedule. **First,** this means leaving our online entertainment world to return to the physical world. **Second,** we can set challenging goals to learn various skills—not only new life skills but also fun skills like cooking, fixing cars, and building or creating something. **Third,** we can take the steps necessary to try different clubs and activities at school or in our local communities.

Building our confidence helps us become independent. Our teenage years are a great time to discover and develop our core values. This is the season when skill, talent, personality, values, and environment come together to form character.

Building confidence enhances our mental health. When we are more sure of our values, our identity gets stronger. We are not as anxious in the face of opposition or peer pressure. We are more stable.

Building confidence involves multiple steps. First, we look to our parents and other caring adults to guide us and not depend on online peers and strangers to tell us who we are. **Second, we surround ourselves with good company.** This step is incredibly important since we tend to become like the people we hang out with. **Third, we look for open-door opportunities** to stretch, get out of our comfort zones, and do gritty things that require hard work and passion.

Just as consistent exercise strengthens our muscles, dedicating effort to developing new skills enhances our confidence. Over time, this growing self-assurance empowers us to share our talents with the world!

STUCK IN SCREEN JAIL

Spending most of our time on screens makes us feel more lonely and anxious. It's easy to feel trapped when screen time is our primary activity. We get locked into a vicious cycle and start spending less time with our communities. This hurts our emotional well-being and mental health. We may feel locked in "screen jail."

SCREENSTRONG KIDS HAVE MORE FREEDOM

When screens are used as a helpful tool rather than our primary source of entertainment, we can shift our focus back to having real-life experiences. Instead of our screens trapping us and keeping us away from the real world, **we will be free to be ourselves and experience better mental health.** Living a ScreenStrong life empowers us to escape "screen jail" and live a more fulfilling, authentic, and healthier life!

WHY YOU NEED TO ESCAPE SCREEN JAIL:

STRESSED
Your brain gets overstimulated from screen overuse, releasing dopamine and stress hormones (adrenaline and cortisol). Feeling stressed and trapped, you can't break free.

SLEEP DEPRIVED
Sleep deprivation causes irritability and fatigue. Exhaustion sets in and often results in bad choices.

LESS MOTIVATED
You lose your motivation for doing meaningful activities that you once enjoyed. The screen is controlling you, but you think you're controlling the screen.

ISOLATED
Spending more time online makes you less connected to those around you. This can result in overwhelming loneliness and depression and also leads to more screen time as the cycle continues.

TRULY CONNECTED
ScreenStrong kids usually have more in-person connections, which leads to a greater sense of belonging and deeper friendships.

MORE PURPOSEFUL
ScreenStrong teens use their skills, gifts, and creativity for good to help people around them. They become purposeful about helping others.

LESS STRESSED
ScreenStrong kids are free from the drama, pressure, and rejection of social media. They are also free from the stress associated with violent video games.

MORE CREATIVE
ScreenStrong teens tend to have more nonscreen interests to share with people. They are more well-rounded and creative in real life.

HAPPIER
According to research, less screen time typically brings a greater sense of life satisfaction. This is partly due to not experiencing the bullying or rejection caused by smartphones or social media and avoiding the loss of purpose from gaming overuse.

HERE ARE SOME SCIENTIFICALLY PROVEN WAYS TO KEEP OUR MENTAL HEALTH IN GOOD SHAPE

1. **Invest in strong relationships** with family and larger communities where we can pursue virtue. For example, belonging to a religious community can be good for our mental health.

2. **Remove addictive screens (social media & video games)** and replace that time with other activities. Replacing high dopamine-producing screen activities with healthy real-world experiences is critical for our mental well-being and overall long-term happiness.

3. **Avoid toxic online content** and toxic people to reduce emotional stress.

4. **Stay physically healthy** by exercising, eating well, and sleeping well.

Living in community, building competence, and growing in confidence can make us less anxious and more fulfilled. Our psychological needs will be met, and **our mental health will be strong enough to resist attacks.**

We will connect more with our families and larger communities as we prepare for deeper friendships, better communication skills, and more social confidence. **Our mental health will be protected when we avoid getting swept away by the online world.**

"Behavior becomes an identity. As a rule, behaving virtuously leads people to become more virtuous."

—Dr. Leonard Sax, MD, PhD, author of *The Collapse of Parenting, Girls on the Edge,* and *Boys Adrift*

SECTION 3
WHAT ARE OTHER TEENS SAYING?

"Read these stories—these kids were so FUR-tunate to learn about ScreenStrong!"

Skippy, The ScreenStrong Cat

Can you relate to any of the following stories?

"I DIDN'T CARE ABOUT ANYTHING."

"When I was little, I loved playing soccer, but music was what I loved most. My parents made me take lessons, and even though I complained at first, I started to really like practicing and learning new songs. I also loved spending time with my friends and my dog. But everything changed when I got my first gaming system in middle school. I was so excited—I could finally play all the games my friends talked about. At first, it was just for fun, but soon, gaming became the only thing I cared about.

I started skipping soccer, and I forgot all about the piano. I even stopped caring about hanging out with my friends or playing with my dog. The only thing that mattered was ranking higher in my game. If I wasn't playing, I was thinking about playing or talking about playing. It was like the game took over my entire brain.

But the worst part? I started getting really mad at the people around me. When I was in the middle of playing, I didn't want anyone to bother me—especially my mom. If she asked me to do something, I would snap. Once, I said something so mean that I saw her eyes well up with tears before she walked away. I knew I had gone too far, but instead of apologizing, I just put my headset back on. That's when my parents decided we were doing a 30-day screen detox—no video games, no social media, no YouTube. I hated the idea. I fought it at first, but they told me there was no way out. The first few days were awful. I was bored, anxious, and angry. But I had to admit—part of me felt relieved.

Without games taking up all my time, I realized I actually missed playing music. I started messing around on the piano again. By the end of the month, I wasn't rushing to get my games back. I realized they were controlling my time. Now I have more time for real things, and everything seems better."

"I FELT MY BODY WASN'T GOOD ENOUGH."

"I started using social media when I was 13. My parents bought me a phone when I was 10, and on my 13th birthday, they let me get social media accounts. It was a day I had looked forward to for a really long time! I was interested in sports and health, so I initially followed fitness influencers. I started eating well and working out, but no matter how hard I tried, I could never look as good as the influencers did.

One of my favorite fitness accounts advised me not to eat if I wasn't hungry. I started worrying about the pounds I would gain if I ate. Soon, I began restricting my portions at each meal. I couldn't help myself! I weighed myself several times a day. If the scale didn't budge, I'd ignore my hunger pangs and not eat. If the number on the scale went up, I would spiral out of control.

Within a few months, my weight had dropped dangerously low, and I was diagnosed with anorexia. My basketball coach refused to let me play on the team because I was fainting at practice. My parents had no idea that all of this was happening, so my coach told me to involve my parents. I finally told them and got help.

My eating disorder is always there in my mind, but with the support of my friends and family, I realize now how toxic social media is for my mental and physical health. I deleted my social media accounts and am playing basketball again, which I love.

I feel so much better, both mentally and physically. I am so thankful my friends and family encouraged me to get off social media, or my life could definitely have been in danger."

"TRAPPED IN THE YOUTUBE LOOP: HOW I BROKE FREE"

"It was no big deal in the beginning. I wanted to learn some cool tricks for my mountain bike, so I searched YouTube for some videos. At first, it was awesome. I found videos on jumps, trails, and how to fix a flat tire. But then, the algorithm started feeding me all kinds of random stuff—funny videos, pranks, and other kids playing video games. I didn't even like watching people play games, but for some reason, I couldn't stop watching.

Hours would pass. Two hours felt like 30 minutes, and my grades started slipping because I wasn't getting my homework done. I told myself I'd only watch one more video, but it never stopped there. It became an endless loop.

The worst part was that the algorithm started showing me inappropriate stuff. Videos I had never searched for would pop up, and even though I knew I shouldn't click, I couldn't help it. The more I clicked, the more they came, and it was like YouTube knew exactly how to keep me hooked. I was starting to get a little depressed.

Then, my family went on a week-long camping trip. No Wi-Fi, no screens—just us, a tent, and lots of nature. At first, I hated it. I kept thinking about the videos I was missing. But by the third day, something clicked. I wasn't distracted anymore, and I realized how much better I felt just being outside and moving! I slept so well under the stars that week. That trip showed me how much control YouTube had over me, and I didn't like it.

When we got home, I talked to my parents about it. They weren't mad. They helped me find and join a mountain biking club for kids my age, so now I'm spending more time on actual trails instead of just watching videos. I also promised them that if I wanted to watch YouTube, I'd do it in the kitchen where they could see so that I wouldn't get sucked into the loop.

Now I am feeling like myself again. Being in the real world on the trail beats watching endless videos any day!"

"I WAS ALWAYS WONDERING IF PEOPLE LIKED ME."

"Have you ever woken up in the morning and checked your phone only to find a bunch of pictures showing a party you weren't invited to? I have, and it hurts.

A year ago, I experienced this and felt an overwhelming amount of FOMO. I sat crying on my bed and thought: 'Why wasn't I invited? Do people not like me? What did I do wrong? Am I not enough?'

I reached out to a friend who I knew was at the party to ask her if she knew why I wasn't invited. She didn't know and tried to reassure me that I didn't miss much. However, I was really hurt. Even though I had spent the evening having fun at my neighbor's pool, I was sad to know I was left out of a get-together that some of my friends had attended. It really made me feel bad about myself.

I talked to my mom and my best friend about it. We talked about how happy I was when I had gone to bed the night before after a fun night of swimming and playing games. Then, I woke up and immediately checked my phone, only to have all the fun I had the night before erased when I knew I had been left out. After much thought and discussion, I decided the best thing to do would be to delete social media from my life. Once I looked deeply into my feelings, I realized that social media seemed fun but really made me feel sad and excluded.

Over this past year, without social media, I've discovered that I was too worried about what other people thought of me. Now I focus on having fun with my real friends in person, and I feel better about myself because I don't see what other people are doing all the time—I can live my REAL life."

"TRYING TO MAKE FRIENDS ON SOCIAL MEDIA DIDN'T WORK."

"When I started middle school, everything changed. My family moved to a new town, and I had to leave behind my friends, my school, and everything I'd known my whole life. I was nervous about making new friends, and after a few weeks of sitting alone at lunch and not really meeting anyone, I started feeling really lonely. That's when I begged my parents to let me get on social media. I thought that if I could connect with my classmates online, it would help me feel included.

At first, it seemed like it was actually helping. I followed kids from my new school, liked their posts, and commented on their pictures. I even started messaging a few of them. Online, some of them responded and seemed friendly, but at school, they barely acknowledged me. It felt like I had friends, but in reality, I was still sitting alone in the cafeteria and walking to class by myself. The more time I spent on social media, the worse I felt. Instead of helping me make real friends, it made me feel even more left out.

After a few months of this, my dad stepped in. He suggested that I stop focusing on social media and start inviting people over instead. I was nervous at first, but I took his advice. I invited a few kids over to watch a baseball game, and to my surprise, they said yes. It turned out that we all loved baseball—watching, playing, and even collecting cards. Over time, those kids became my real friends.

Now, we hang out all the time. We play baseball together, trade cards, and have way more fun than I ever did scrolling on my phone. Looking back, I wish I had never turned to social media. Making real friends in person is so much better. I'm glad I figured that out before I wasted more time!"

"I COULDN'T STOP PLAYING FORTNITE.*"*

"It started as just a fun way to hang out with my friends online, but before I knew it, *Fortnite* was taking over my life. I was lying to my parents, skipping homework, and staying up all night playing. I couldn't stop thinking about it—even during school. I was just counting down the minutes until I could get back to my room and log on.

It got so bad that I barely talked to my family anymore. I stopped going outside, quit hanging out with friends in real life, and my grades were tanking. But none of that mattered to me then because I just wanted to play. *Fortnite* owned me.

Then my mom stepped in. She saw what was happening and made me quit completely. I was furious. I argued, begged, and even told her she was ruining my life. But after a few days without the game, something weird happened—I started feeling better. I slept more, I wasn't constantly stressed about getting back online, and my brain felt clearer.

With all my free time, I picked up an old hobby I had forgotten about—drawing. At first, it was just something to do, but then I really got into it. Now, I've been asked to participate in a big art project our school is sponsoring at a homeless shelter. I never thought I'd be excited about something like that, but I am.

Looking back, I can't believe how much time I wasted in my room playing a game that didn't actually matter. Being around my friends, creating art, and getting out of the house is so much more fun than *Fortnite* ever was—I just didn't realize it when I was stuck in that loop.

If you're a gamer, I get it. It's hard to imagine life without it. It seems like the only fun thing in the world. But trust me—there are so many better things out there. You'll never regret making real memories with your friends."

"I WILL NEVER LOOK AS GOOD AS MY FRIENDS."

"Social media made it so hard not to compare myself to everyone else. Every time I opened Instagram or Snapchat, there were pictures of my friends looking perfect and confident, like they had everything figured out. It wasn't just them—it was the influencers and celebrities, too. I'd scroll through photos of chopstick-legged supermodels, perfectly edited and posed, and think, *Why can't I look like that?* It felt like no matter what I did, I was never enough.

It got to the point where I couldn't even look at myself in the mirror without seeing everything I hated. My self-esteem was horrible, and I didn't even realize how much of it was coming from my phone. I didn't see how it was damaging me.

When I finally got rid of my smartphone, everything changed. At first, I was nervous—I thought I'd feel left out or miss knowing what everyone was up to. But the opposite happened. Without constant notifications pulling me back, I stopped thinking about filters, likes, or how my body looked compared to someone else's.

For the first time in a long time, I felt actually confident. I could focus on more important things than trying to look 'perfect' for an audience of people who probably weren't even paying that much attention. I started feeling good about myself just as I was.

Now, I'm actually happy to be off my phone. I'm not trapped in that cycle of comparison anymore, and the freedom to not care about looking perfect is such a relief."

"SOCIAL MEDIA MADE ME QUIT FOOTBALL."

"I was so excited when my Mom and Dad gave me a smartphone for my 13th birthday. I slowly started adding apps and choosing new websites to visit. Soon, I was spending more time on my phone than anything else—except playing football. My Dad was a career athlete, so I was really happy to follow in his footsteps. From the time I was in kindergarten, I spent every minute I could strengthening my football skills—throwing, catching, and running routes. When I got to high school, I started on the Varsity team as a 10th grader. I was so pumped. I was able to train as the team's quarterback and spent hours on throwing lessons and working hard in the gym.

Halfway through the summer between 10th and 11th grade, I found out that college scouts would discuss players' stats and abilities on Twitter. I got SO ADDICTED to checking up on all the players I knew would be competing against me. Then, I had the idea to see what these coaches and scouts were saying about me.

At first, this really boosted my confidence. They were saying so many positive things—but then, it happened. I had a game in October of my junior year when I was just 'off' (probably from all the sleep I was losing, staying up late on my phone). I threw three interceptions, and the other team scored two TDs on my mistakes. After the game, my poor performance was all over Twitter. I was so devastated that I could not get over it for weeks. This was all I could think about. I ended up having to quit the team because I couldn't play without intense anxiety.

Now, as a senior, after a lot of therapy and hard work, I am back on the team as the starting quarterback. However, I made one huge change that has made the biggest difference—NO MORE SOCIAL MEDIA! If you are a middle school or high school athlete, I strongly recommend staying smartphone free as long as possible. You won't regret it!"

"BREAKING FREE FROM THE TIKTOK TRAP"

"I started posting my dance routines on TikTok in 8th grade because it seemed like a fun way to share what I love. At first, it was exciting. I got likes, comments, and followers, which made me feel so good—like I was getting noticed for something I was proud of. But then things got weird. Strangers started leaving comments that didn't feel right. Some of them were really inappropriate, and I didn't even know these people.

I told myself it wasn't a big deal, but I couldn't stop thinking about it. I'd keep checking my account, feeling this mix of excitement and dread. The attention was addicting, but the creepy messages made my stomach hurt. I felt trapped like I couldn't stop posting because I didn't want to lose my followers, but at the same time, I hated the way it made me feel.

I didn't tell my parents because I was embarrassed and didn't want them to take my phone away. But the anxiety started affecting everything—my dancing, my friendships, even how I got along with my mom. I felt like I was carrying this huge secret, which was stressful. Then, one night, everything changed. My mom went to this talk about screens and kids, and when she came home, she asked me how I was feeling about my phone. I didn't want to answer at first, but I could tell she wasn't mad, so I just told her everything. I cried so much, but it felt so good to finally say it out loud.

She didn't yell at me or blame me. Instead, she helped me delete my TikTok account and get a basic phone, one that could just call and text people. At first, it was hard, but now I feel so free. I don't have to worry about comments or followers anymore. My mom and I are so much closer now, and I have fun dancing again. I even invite my friends to practice routines at my house after school. I'm so glad that chapter of my life is done—I'm just so much happier now."

BRIGHTER DAYS AHEAD!

We've been where you are—stuck in the cycle of endless scrolling, video games, and social media. We thought we couldn't live without it, but we were wrong.

We broke free from toxic screens, and what we found was life-changing—stronger family connections, real friendships, better grades, more confidence, and **time to actually enjoy life**.

We're not here to judge you or tell you what to do. We're here to show you that it's possible because we've done it. We've faced the fear of missing out, the pressure to stay connected, and we've come out stronger. **If you're struggling, feeling overwhelmed, or just wondering if there's more to life than a screen—you're not alone.**

We'll point you to everything you need to be ScreenStrong through high school: resources, support, and a community that gets it. You don't have to stay stuck. Be bold. Be different. **Be ScreenStrong.**

CAN YOU REMEMBER?

1. Your parents don't allow smartphones or video games because:

- ☐ They are old and don't understand why you love screens so much.
- ☐ They are mad at you for teasing your little brother all the time.
- ☐ They talked to some other parents who hate screens.
- ☐ They wish they were more popular on social media.
- ☐ They know that research says that excessive screen time hurts young brains.

2. It is not uncommon for rejection pain to come from our closest friends:

- ☐ True
- ☐ False

3. Gaming and social media are not healthy hobbies because:

- ☐ They can quickly become addictive.
- ☐ They can replace time spent focusing on meaningful interests.
- ☐ They can expose us to bad influences.
- ☐ They can increase our anxiety.
- ☐ All of the above

WHAT I CAN DO TODAY TO HAVE MORE EMOTIONAL FREEDOM FROM MY SCREENS?

- ☐ I will avoid social media and video games.
- ☐ I will make a list of hobbies to try.
- ☐ I will encourage my friends to try a new hobby, extracurricular, or sports activity with me.
- ☐ I will use a voice/text phone and make sure to call my friends more.
- ☐ Every day this week, I will make a point of reading a book, meeting up with friends after school, and going outside to get some exercise.

CHAPTER SEVEN

FREEDOM FROM ELEPHANTS

CHAPTER 7: INTRODUCTION
FREEDOM FROM ELEPHANTS

Welcome to Chapter Seven.

Let's get real: technology gives us access to incredible things—amazing ways to learn, connect, and explore the world. But it also opens a door to some seriously dark and harmful things, and pornography is one of the worst.

Porn is everywhere and pushed like it's no big deal, but the truth is, it damages your brain, relationships, and future. It's not harmless entertainment; it's addictive and designed to hook you.

Talking about porn can feel awkward, but avoiding the topic only makes it more dangerous. This chapter isn't here to shame you—it's here to help you understand how porn hijacks your brain and why it's a trap. Knowing the truth will help you avoid the damage, take control, and confidently talk about it with those who can help you.

Here's what we'll tackle in this chapter:

1. *What happens in your brain when you see a pornographic image?*
2. *Why is porn so addictive, and how does it trap people?*
3. *What can you do to avoid the porn trap and stay strong?*

Let's face the truth and learn how to live smarter and stronger.

Adam

"The cat's out of the bag! Our brains save every image they see FUR-ever, especially when they are graphic, novel, or violent. Be very careful what you watch."

Skippy, The ScreenStrong Cat

PORNOGRAPHY: the elephant in the room

In the previous chapters, we discussed what it means to overuse our screens and how that can hurt our brains. Two of the most significant issues with screen use include **how much time we spend** on them and **what content we view**. **Pornography** is a big part of the problem with harmful content.

WHAT IS PORN?

Porn (pornography) refers to pictures, videos, or cartoons of people with little or no clothing on, appearing to engage in sexual activity. These images and videos are often staged and edited, making them exaggerated, unrealistic, and oftentimes even violent. Watching porn gives people misleading ideas about relationships and can negatively affect mental health.

Note: Scientific images of body parts, such as those in your science textbook, are not considered porn.

WHY IS PORNOGRAPHY SO ADDICTIVE AND HARMFUL?

Humans experience the highest dopamine release from two natural sources: eating and reproduction. This makes sense since food is essential for survival, and reproduction is necessary for the continuation of the human species.

Our brains also respond strongly to what we see on screens. For example, they react to video game violence in the same way they would to real-life violence. The same applies to pornography. When viewing sexual images, the brain perceives them as real, which triggers a large release of dopamine. The problem with this, however, goes beyond being just another addiction; it distorts how we view people and what we consider healthy relationships.

Let's dive deeper into how inappropriate sexual images are tied to our brain's reward system.

Our BRAINS love REWARDS

The emotion center—also called the reward center—is an area of the brain located in the **ventral striatum,** in the middle. This is where dopamine is activated and where the hippocampus (the memory center) is located. So we not only feel good about what we are doing, but the hippocampus helps us **remember why we feel good** so that we will repeat the rewarding activity.

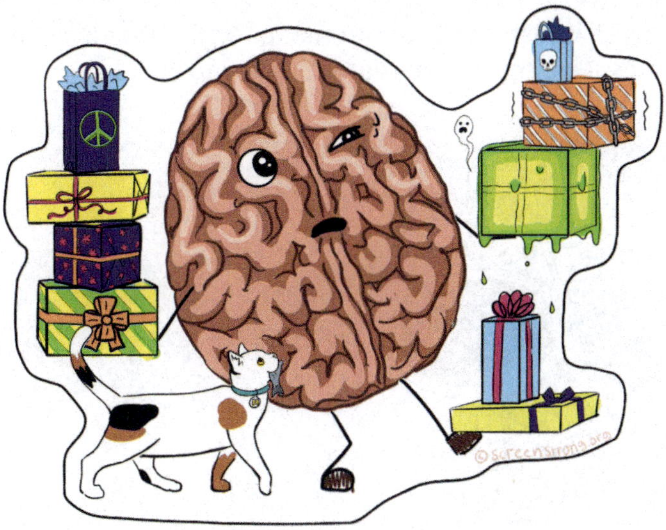

Rewards can be either healthy or unhealthy.

Our brains are wired to seek rewards—both healthy and unhealthy. We feel good when we enjoy a delicious meal, but unhealthy stimuli trigger the same reward system. Activities like gambling, endless social media scrolling, or consuming highly stimulating content—including inappropriate material—can hijack the brain's reward center, making it hard to break free.

Since our brains are designed to crave all rewards, it's up to us to focus on healthy rewards and avoid the unhealthy ones.

HEALTHY REWARDS LEAD TO GOOD HABITS.

The reward area in our brains gets activated by many things, such as hanging out with friends, playing sports, reading, doing challenging puzzles, exercising, and playing the piano. **Healthy rewards don't negatively affect our lives**; they make them more fun and fulfilling.

Healthy rewards can often improve our relationships with others, our health, our motivation, and our lives. Healthy rewards are the way to go!

UNHEALTHY REWARDS LEAD TO BAD HABITS.

Some rewards aren't good for us, but our brains still crave them anyway. Using drugs is an example of an unhealthy reward. Playing video games, binge-watching YouTube videos, scrolling through social media, and viewing porn are all examples of unhealthy rewards. Unfortunately, these activities are designed to release excessive dopamine, making them much more addictive than healthy rewards. **The more dopamine an activity triggers, the higher the chance it will become addictive.**

But porn isn't just another high-dopamine activity—it's uniquely harmful. Unlike other addictions, it distorts your view of relationships, fuels the exploitation of others, and can lead to compulsive behaviors that are hard to break. **Its impact goes beyond addiction, affecting both you and others in serious, lasting ways.**

DRAW A LINE FROM THE ACTIVITIES LISTED ON THE RIGHT TO THE TYPE OF REWARD ON THE LEFT.

Decide if the following rewards are **healthy** or **unhealthy**:

HEALTHY REWARDS

UNHEALTHY REWARDS

Reading

Eating too much sugar

Hanging out with friends

Using illegal drugs

Exercising

Drinking too much alcohol

Listening to good music

Viewing inappropriate online images and videos

Playing video games

Eating healthy food

Using social media

Viewing violent online content

when UNHEALTHY REWARDS take over our BRAINS

Addiction happens when unhealthy rewards take over the reward pathway in our brains, and the **reward center becomes out of balance.**

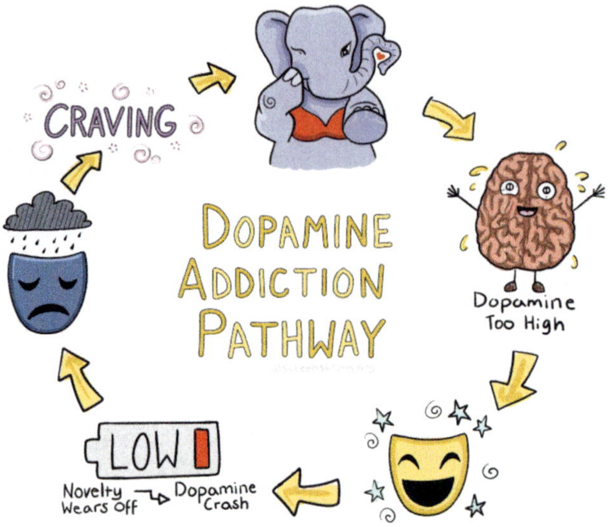

STEPS TO A PORN ADDICTION

1. **High dopamine.** Viewing porn triggers higher-than-normal dopamine levels.

2. **Novelty wears off.** Over time, our brains get bored with the same images, so the level of dopamine drops.

3. **Feelings of sadness.** We feel sad because now we have less dopamine.

4. **Craving.** We remember where we got a good feeling, so we search for more porn.

5. **New material.** Now we need new, different, and often more extreme pornographic pictures or videos to get the same level of dopamine. We seek out more novel content, and the cycle continues. We hate it, but we are stuck in a trap.

PORN IS NOT A JOKE.
IT'S A VERY BIG DEAL.

Pornography is not a neutral activity.

Porn images are very influential. Just as food changes our bodies, the **images we see change our brains**, what we think, and how we perceive the world around us.

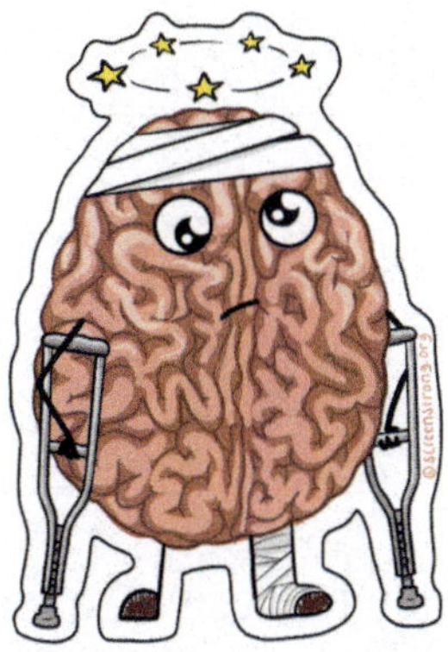

Porn confuses our values.

Viewing inappropriate images mixes up the reward system in our brains. Now, healthy activities don't seem as fun anymore. But it gets worse. When we start associating rewards with something harmful, our brains get confused and think the harmful thing is good for us.

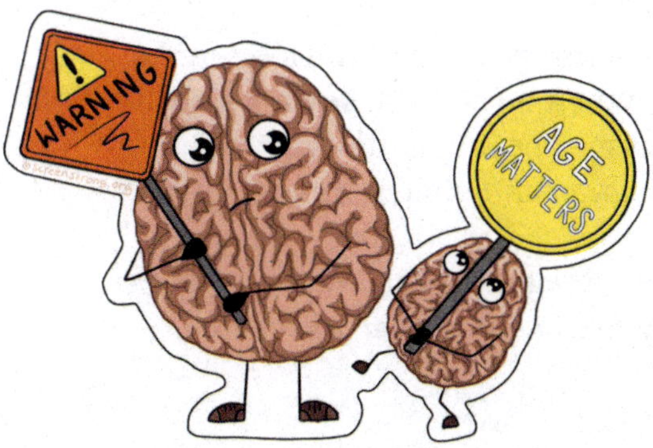

Porn damages young brains the most.

Porn is especially harmful when we are young because our brains are still developing and are highly impressionable.

As we learned in Chapter One, when specific learning pathways are paved early, they tend to stay that way. Changing them later in life is possible but much more difficult.

We can learn the right things well, but we can also learn the wrong things well. This is how bad habits are formed.

Therefore, if someone develops a habit of viewing porn as a teen, it can be harder to break later in life. **This will negatively impact self-perception, including future relationships with your spouse and your family.**

"Things that are crazy seem normal if you say, see, and do them long enough. When it comes to 'elephants,' that's just CLAW-ful!"

Skippy, The ScreenStrong Cat

how PORN gets STUCK in our BRAINS

In Chapter Three, we explored the workings of the visual cortex. Now we will see **how negative images impact our brains**, shape our thoughts, and change our perceptions of the world.

Like files on a memory chip, **the brain stores every image seen** in the long-term memory center for future recall. This is beneficial when it comes to storing positive memories and healthy pictures and content. It becomes problematic when we expose ourselves to toxic content, such as pornographic and violent images.

Unfortunately, we can't just decide to keep the good images and delete the bad ones from our brains. **However, we can decide what we allow our eyes to see.**

Pornography is a serious subject. We can't hide the effects by keeping it a secret and not talking about it.

OUR BRAINS STORE EVERY IMAGE WE SEE

Because pornography harms our brains, keeping our brains clean and clear of toxic images will help us have healthier brains.

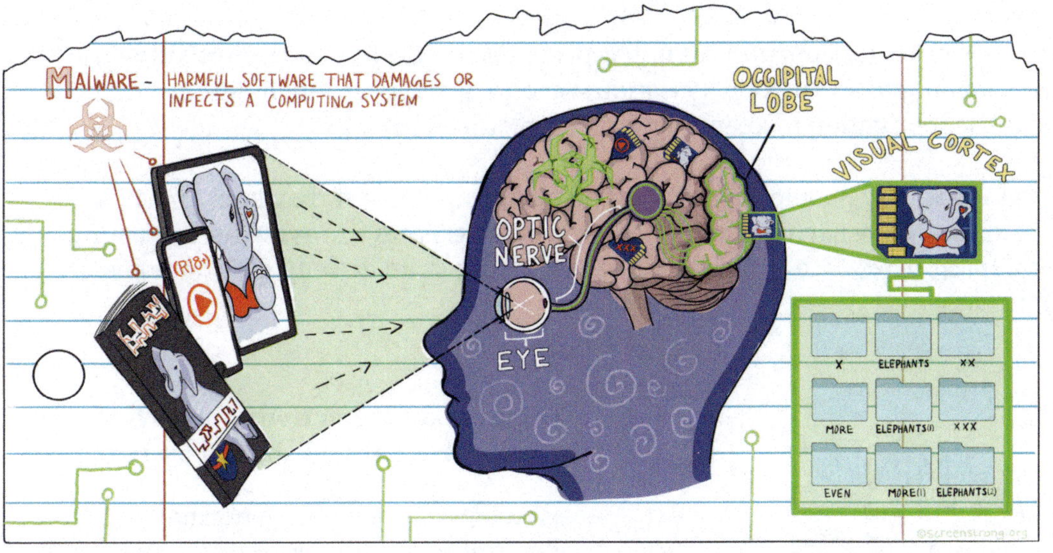

PERMANENT RECORDINGS
Memories in our brains don't get cleaned out. Most people don't realize that every image we see is permanently recorded in our brains.

LONG-TERM MEMORY
Any memory recalled after 30 seconds is in the long-term memory. Every image we see is permanently recorded in long-term memory center in our brains.

CRAVINGS
The more porn we see, the more we may seek it. Viewing porn images create a craving for more porn, even if we don't like it.

UNLIMITED STORAGE
It has been estimated that the average adult brain can accumulate the equivalent of 2.5 million gigabytes of memory. That's a lot!

STRUCTURAL CHANGES
Brain changes occur in response to repeated mental experiences. This includes things we see and think about over and over again, good or bad. Repeated pleasure experiences in the reward center are one of the strongest drivers of change. Porn viewing stimulates excess dopamine in the reward center, changing the structure of the brain, just like a substance addiction.

DAMAGED FUTURE
Viewing the wrong way to do something over and over will eventually change our thinking. Porn can influence poor and unacceptable behaviors toward others, especially women. Regardless of the age of exposure, porn images distort views of healthy relationships.

WILLPOWER AND DECISION-MAKING
Porn can affect our brains in a way that's similar to harmful computer viruses or malware. When we're exposed to it repeatedly, the part of our brain that controls decision-making and willpower can get weaker.

Over time, this can rewire our brain to crave porn, making it harder to focus on real relationships and healthy choices.

WHY DO WE CRAVE SOMETHING WE DON'T WANT TO DO?

Dopamine serves two purposes. First, it provides the **thrill of accomplishing** the activity, leading to a feel-good sensation. Second, it **triggers our memory** and gives us the motivation to keep doing it, setting up a craving.

The craving is why people get stuck in the porn trap. Even if they know porn is bad for them, the rewiring of their reward center creates a craving for it, turning it into a habit. They face a big challenge: persisting in an activity they do not wish to continue.

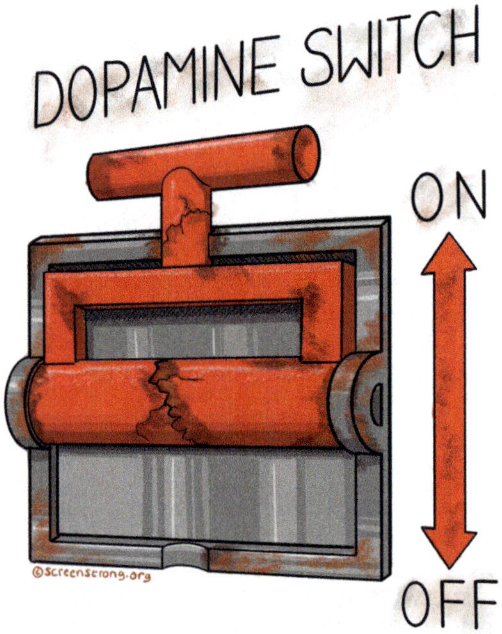

High-dopamine activities override the brain's natural shutoff system.

When we eat a meal—a normal dopamine-producing activity—the brain signals that we are full and to stop eating. However, activities that release high amounts of dopamine cause decreased activity in the frontal cortex—the part of the brain responsible for signaling when to stop.

Over time, this continual impact wears down the frontal cortex, and the shutoff system breaks—the switch gets stuck in the ON position. This is one reason why it is difficult to control the porn habit.

To put it simply, watching porn can quickly become a powerful addiction. Like speeding downhill with failed brakes, it can spiral out of control, leading to serious consequences. If not stopped, the compulsive urge to seek out inappropriate images can rewire the brain and wreak havoc on our lives, now and for years to come.

FRONTAL CORTEX DAMAGE

The frontal cortex is crucial for decision-making and impulse control. Exposure to harmful content can impair this area of the brain, **making it harder to think clearly and regulate actions.** This increases the likelihood of making poor decisions.

DAMAGE TO THE REWARD CENTER

When the brain is overstimulated by content that is sexual, it becomes accustomed to intense dopamine surges. As a result, **everyday activities that once felt enjoyable may start to seem dull,** less rewarding, or even depressing.

LESS GRAY MATTER

Some studies show that over time, people who view a lot of pornography have **less gray matter in their brains.** Remember, gray matter is a type of brain tissue that allows us to function normally every day. *(Review Chapter One).*

CUMULATIVE EFFECT OF PORN

The damage from repeated exposure adds up over time, with each experience leaving a lasting impact. Our brains don't reset each day, so every exposure has significance.

Fortunately, healing can start as soon as the harmful habit is discontinued.

"I was on my phone just researching something for biology class and ended up, two clicks later, on a porn site. It was so fascinating to me that I couldn't stop looking at it. I finally told my parents about it and they helped me stop. But it was surprising how quickly it became a shameful part of my life."

—13-year-old boy

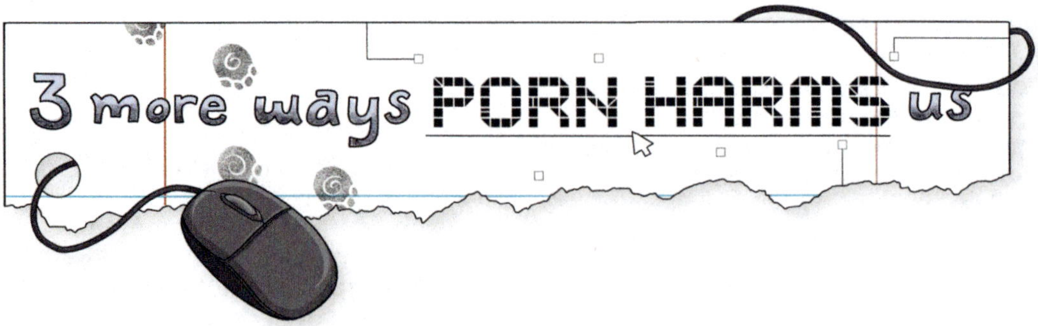

Most people agree that there are moral reasons that viewing violent and toxic content like pornography is wrong. However, there are other reasons you should be careful about what types of photos and videos you allow in your brain. Dr. Adriana Stacey is a doctor who understands mental health. She says:

"Scientific studies show that young men and women who view pornography report severe levels of depression, anxiety, and stress as opposed to their peers who are not viewers of this type of media. Pornography preys on the addictive centers in your brain, which can lead to cravings and other symptoms of addiction. Then, when you try to stop watching, the brain tends to fight back, which can lead to more severe mental health issues. The best first step is to not ever start watching porn, but if you already have, now is the time to stop!"

1. PORN HARMS OUR MENTAL HEALTH

Studies show that the more porn someone views, the more likely they will be to experience mental health issues such as anxiety and depression. Depression can be one of the first signs of a porn habit. Here are some others:

2. PORN HARMS OUR RELATIONSHIPS

Pornography causes **distorted views** about people (especially women) and intimate relationships between people (sex). It also causes a distorted view of ourselves and how we think about our own bodies.

3. PORN HARMS OUR MOTIVATION

A porn habit can cause us to be less interested in the activities we used to enjoy. When our brains get used to high dopamine levels from unhealthy activities, other things that used to bring us joy are less attractive.

It is best to never start watching porn, but if you already have, now is the time to stop!

How do smart kids like us fall into the quicksand?

Our introduction to pornography is usually accidental. We clicked on a link by mistake, or maybe a friend showed us something on a phone at school, in the tree house, or at a sleepover.

At first, we feel strange and embarrassed. Unfortunately, it's hard to stop looking because **our brains are wired to seek out novel and unusual things.** What begins as curiosity can quickly turn into something much harder to break free from.

Over time, watching pornography can become an unhealthy pattern that's tough to stop. Let's learn more about how this behavior starts and continues.

1. ACCESS INCREASES WITH SMALL SCREENS.
We have more access when we get a tablet or smartphone. With more screen privacy comes more problems.

3. WE ARE EMBARRASSED.
We feel like we can't tell anyone so we don't get help. We begin to get caught in a cycle of viewing more porn.

5. THE ALGORITHM KICKS IN.
If we accidentally click on one sexual image, then the algorithm will be set to send us more, even when we don't search for it. The elephant is now in the room; data is working against us, and it becomes hard to get rid of the elephant.

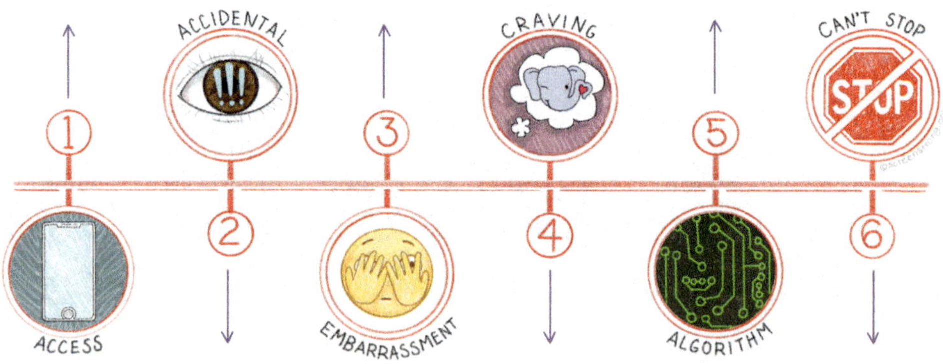

2. ACCIDENTAL EXPOSURE HAPPENS.
We are not searching for porn, but it appears when searching for something else. Just because it is accidental doesn't make it less damaging.

4. CRAVINGS ARE FORMED.
Dopamine is high, a craving is formed, and the habit is now established. A porn habit that started young is strong. New habits are built.

6. ADDICTION STARTS.
We start to lose control over our habits. We think we can stop, but we can't. We begin to feel pretty bad but don't know how to escape the trap.

MORE REASONS IT'S EASY TO GET STUCK

Everyone was talking about a word at school, and you didn't know what it meant, so you went home and searched for it online. You were curious. You didn't mean to see what you saw. You didn't mean to get caught in the porn trap.

You used to play outside all the time, but when you got a smartphone for your birthday, you were on your phone all the time instead.

At the sleepover, everyone was looking at porn and laughing, so you wanted to see it, too. You felt embarrassed, but you had a hard time not looking.

When you were younger, you told your parents everything. Now that you're older, you get more embarrassed. You don't want to disappoint them, so you keep secrets.

When the basketball season ended, you had nothing to do after school, so you went to your room and started killing time on your screen.

Because kids' and teenagers' brains are more changeable than adult brains, they are more vulnerable to lasting damage from bad influences and images. Starting a porn habit at a young age is a problem because it can **negatively affect the way our brains are wired.**

Fortunately, there is good news. Even though young brains are susceptible to bad influences, they can also start new habits easily. When we stop viewing porn, the porn pathways will begin to fade. **We can make significant changes now when we are young that will save our future brains.**

BE CAREFUL WHAT YOU SEARCH FOR
THE ALGORITHM FOLLOWS YOU

What Happens When You Search Online

Have you ever searched for something online and then noticed that similar things keep popping up afterward? That's because of something called an algorithm. We learned about algorithms on page 46. It is like a secret computer program that remembers what you search for and uses that information to show you more of the same type of content. For example, if you search for basketball highlights, the algorithm will think, "Oh, they like basketball!" and send more basketball videos your way.

But here's the tricky part: **if you accidentally search for something inappropriate or click on a video or website with sexual content, the algorithm doesn't know it was a mistake.** It will still assume you're interested in that kind of content and start showing you more of it. Even if you delete your search history, the algorithm remembers what you typed and keeps serving you similar stuff. It's also a good idea to be super careful about what words you type into search engines. Even one word can lead to inappropriate content being shown to you later. This can feel over-whelming and scary, but it's important to remember—you're not stuck!

What Should You Do?

If you ever stumble across sexual content or something that feels wrong, the best thing to do is tell your parents or a trusted adult right away. They won't be mad at you for something you didn't mean to find—they'll help you fix it. Parents can block the bad content and adjust settings so the algorithm stops sending it to you.

"Stay away from temptations and stay PAW-sitive!"
Skippy, The ScreenStrong Cat

It's hard for the human brain to resist **temptation** when something is right in front of us. **The closer we are to temptation, the weaker we get.** Therefore, the best way to stop a porn habit is to get as far away from the temptation as we can. The further away we are, the stronger our discipline and willpower will be. That is simple to understand but sometimes very hard to figure out in real life.

"Disciplined people are better at structuring their lives in a way that does not require heroic willpower and self-control. In other words, they spend less time in tempting situations."

— James Clear, author of *Atomic Habits*

Unfortunately, porn can be an invisible problem during the teen years because of its isolating and private nature. It is also a threat to our emotional health, so we need to learn the best ways to avoid the porn trap now.

What we do now really matters because, during adolescence, our brains are being molded for the future.

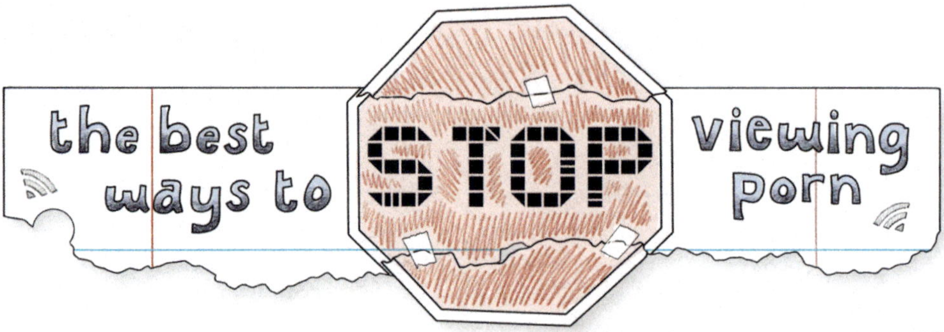

TALK TO YOUR PARENTS

A porn habit can only survive in secret. **When you talk about it and have accountability, it loses power.** Kids and teens who talk openly with their parents or trusted adults and learn about the dangers of porn are less likely to get caught in the porn trap than kids who keep secrets from their parents. Research shows that everyone wins when we work together with our parents as a team to avoid exposure.

TIP: *Are you curious about a sexual word you heard? Don't Google it or ask a friend; ask your parents instead. Your parents and other trusted adults in your life care about you more than the internet does, and they have more wisdom than your friends, so let them help you with this.*

REMOVE ACCESS

Research shows that removing all access to an unwanted habit is the most effective way to break it. **The best way to stop looking at pornography is to eliminate easy access to devices where it's readily available.** Since over 80% of pornography is viewed on smartphones, many teens are choosing non-data, voice/text-only phones to regain control and break the pornography habit. Think of it like trying to stop eating donuts—you wouldn't keep them on the kitchen counter if you wanted to resist. The same goes for breaking free from the porn trap: we have to remove access to the source!

TIP: *Use a talk/text phone that has no internet connection. These basic phones still allow you to call and text your friends, but you won't have to worry about unwanted sexual content from the internet.*

DON'T USE SCREENS IN PRIVATE PLACES

When we must use our screens for homework, we should use them out in the open and on larger screens. That makes it much easier to stay away from porn. **Using our screens in private when no one is around is never a good thing.** We can easily end up somewhere online that we don't want to be. Remember, no secrets.

TIP: Never take your screens into your bedroom (or bathroom). Do your screen homework in an open area like the kitchen, where you won't be as tempted to click on inappropriate links and images.

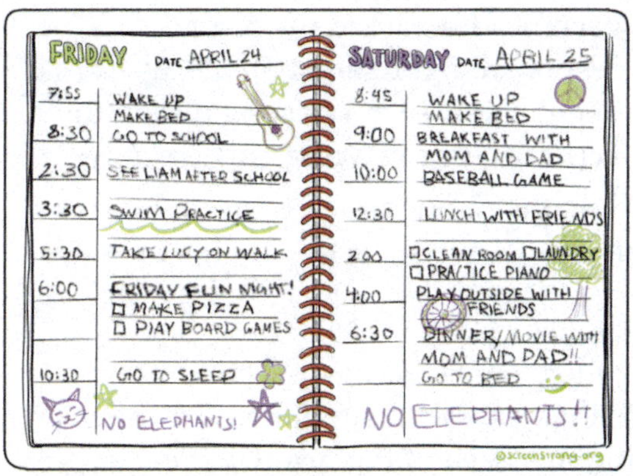

FILL YOUR DOWNTIME WITH GOOD THINGS

We are at a greater risk of seeing porn when we are bored, isolated, and lonely, so keeping ourselves busy with healthy activities is important. **Fill extra time with productive hobbies and in-person time with friends.** We can't wait for parents to do this for us. Physical exercise and going outside will also help us fill the empty time that may lead to too much free time on screens.

TIP: Make a schedule every day. Discover a new hobby or sign up for an after-school sport or club activity so you aren't tempted to fill your time viewing porn.

USE FILTERING SOFTWARE

The right filtering software will help keep elephants off our screens. **Filtering is not perfect, but it will block a lot of unwanted content.** It's like wearing a seatbelt when we are in the car. We may still have a wreck, but the seatbelt may save our lives.

TIP: Ask your parents to install a filter on all the devices in your house. If porn is still getting through, ask them to upgrade it. See filter recommendations at ScreenStrong.org.

GIVE YOUR FRONTAL CORTEX A WORKOUT

When we strengthen our frontal cortex—the part of the brain responsible for self-control—we become better at resisting unhealthy activities like viewing pornography. A weak frontal cortex makes it harder to think ahead and make wise choices. Our goal is to build the ability to pause, think, and choose long-term benefits over instant gratification.

Activities like doing puzzles and playing strategy board games, practicing mindfulness, limiting multi-tasking, and setting goals with small rewards help build executive function skills, strengthening this area of the brain. Other ways include increasing face-to-face social interactions and engaging in sports and activities like drawing, writing, or playing a musical instrument. These help strengthen cognitive flexibility and problem-solving skills. Patience is key—strengthening this part of our brains takes time, and we'll need our parents' support along the way.

TIP: See Chapter Two (executive functioning skills) for ways to strengthen the front of your brain.

ACCOUNTABILITY

THE TRUSTED ADULTS IN YOUR LIFE—PARENTS, MENTORS, AND GUARDIANS—ARE HERE TO SUPPORT YOU.

One of the best ways to stay safe from harmful content online is to have accountability so that you have others helping you. Right now, the best accountability partners are the trusted adults in your life—parents, mentors, and guardians. They have your back and want the best for you online, just like they do in every other area of your life. Think about it: When you were learning to ride a bike, they ensured you wore a helmet. When you started swimming, they stayed close to keep you safe. The internet is no different.

Having your parents or trusted adults in your life as accountability partners means they can help you make smart choices, avoid dangerous situations, and stay on track with the values that matter most to you and your family. You don't have to figure this out alone—the trusted adults in your life are here to support and protect you.

It's also important to know that a lot of the content in pornography is not just inappropriate—it's illegal. Many videos involve people who are being exploited or trafficked, meaning they were forced into it against their will. Watching these videos fuels an industry built on harm and abuse. Just like stealing or cheating, supporting something illegal—whether on purpose or by accident—has real consequences. That's why laws exist to keep kids away from this harmful material and why the trusted adults in your life are helping to protect you from something that can have lasting negative effects.

TIP: *We can't do it alone. We need our parents and other trusted adults in our lives to keep us accountable. They care about us the most.*

NOTES

TIP: Want to win the porn battle? Go here to learn about ideas for basic phones and filters. We have your back!

PHONE & FILTERS

CAN YOU REMEMBER?

1. What happens when a porn image enters your brain?

- ☐ The image disappears from your brain after 30 seconds.
- ☐ It is stored permanently in your brain like a file on a memory chip.
- ☐ It gets stuck in your eye and never enters your brain.
- ☐ The porn image will disappear once you tell it to go away.

2. What are some reasons kids get caught in the porn trap?

- ☐ Access on a screen
- ☐ Curiosity
- ☐ Peer pressure
- ☐ Boredom
- ☐ All of the above

3. How do you avoid the porn trap?

- ☐ Wear dark sunglasses so you can't see as well.
- ☐ Practice by having porn up on your computer and looking away.
- ☐ Spend less time in tempting situations.
- ☐ Take a trip to Mars because they don't have the internet there yet.

HERE IS A LIST OF SOME THINGS YOU CAN DO TO KEEP YOUR BRAIN PORN FREE:

- ☐ Ask your parents to **replace your smartphone** with a phone that doesn't have the internet.
- ☐ Ask your parents to **get parental controls** on any screen you can access (laptop, school tablet, smart TV). Parental controls aren't perfect, but they help. Do not try to hack parental controls and filters to work around your parents' protection. They are trying to help you, not hurt you.
- ☐ **Never take your small screens to your bedroom** or any other private place. You will be more tempted if you do.
- ☐ Find a friend to have as an **accountability partner** and both agree to choose to have a porn-free life. It helps when you know someone else has the same high standard as you.
- ☐ **Ask your parents about porn** when you have questions. They know more than your friends and love and care for you unconditionally. We know it takes courage now, but when you are in high school, you will be so happy you can have open conversations with them.

NOTES

CHAPTER EIGHT

YOUR ADVENTURE AWAITS

CHAPTER 8: INTRODUCTION YOUR ADVENTURE AWAITS

Welcome to Chapter Eight.

Now that you know how screens affect you, it's time to take what you've learned and start a new chapter—literally in this book and also in your life! Here's a quick recap of what this book has taught you so far:

Not all screen time is bad, but the screens that cause the most dopamine—like video games and social media—are the most harmful as they distract us from better things. The natural world is a winner for building stronger friendships and a healthier brain. The more time you spend on screens, the less time you have for the real world, and the higher the risk of poor health.

Your brain is creating habits for the future, which is why now is the best time to explore new hobbies and interests. Living the ScreenStrong way gives you the freedom to explore, make real friends, and have more fun in the real world!

This book has given you knowledge that most people don't have, putting you one step ahead of the crowd. By choosing the ScreenStrong pathway, you're avoiding the trap of screen overuse—and trust me, it's worth it. My friends and I know firsthand that living without those distractions opens the door to a much better life.

Enjoy your new adventure!

Lydia

"With the right CAT-itude, anything is PAWS-ible!
You can be ScreenStrong like me!"
Skippy, The ScreenStrong Cat

A NEW ADVENTURE

Being different takes courage, but you can do it!

By giving your brain the time to develop and grow in healthy ways, you are empowering yourself to have deeper friendships, do more exciting things, and have more genuine experiences. Becoming a ScreenStrong Teen sets you apart from the crowd that is caught in the screen trap. Instead of following the culture, you and your ScreenStrong friends can **enjoy creating your own culture**.

Now that you know how your brain works, you can focus on strengthening it. **And strong brains can change the world!**

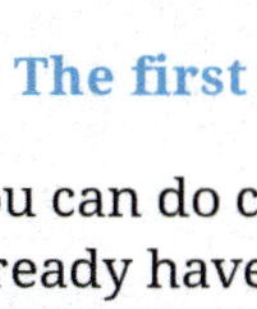

"Being different is great! It might seem hard at first, but once you get used to it, being different is a ton of fun. By standing out from the crowd, you'll become confident in your own skin. And soon, others will start to want to be different with you."
—Andrew, ScreenStrong Teen

The first step is to change your environment and remove the problem.

You can do certain things to make your escape from screen jail easier. Maybe you already have a smartphone or a gaming console, or maybe you don't, but the first step is the same either way. It's the same first step that is necessary to prevent addiction or stop a bad habit.

CREATE A NEW ENVIRONMENT

@screenstrong.org

Your Bedroom

Breaking free from any bad habit requires a change of environment. Changing your environment involves changing routines and physically removing the things that trigger the habit you are trying to stop. **It also includes putting things in place to ensure that good choices are more accessible.**

Removing video games and smartphones from your bedroom will allow you to develop new healthy habits and have time to learn more hobbies. Make your bedroom your own space. Rearrange your furniture, hang up your favorite posters, or display a collection. There are so many ways to make a space your own. Even if you share your room, you can still make changes to it.

On the next page you can get ideas for making your bedroom a place where making good choices is easy. This is just a start. **The possibilities are endless!**

BEDROOM IDEAS:

PHOTOS OF FRIENDS
Print photos of your friends and display them in your room. Keep a photo album in your room.

NEW PAINT COLORS
Paint your room! Ask your parents if you can paint your room, or just one wall, a new color, or try removable wallpaper.

MUSIC
Fill your room with music with a non-data MP3, radio, or speakers—no need for headphones!

A NEAT BED
Studies show that people who make their beds every morning are more successful in life. Starting your day with one successful activity sets you on a great pathway for the whole day.

PRIVATE DIARY OR JOURNAL
Writing down our thoughts in a private place is important for our mental health. Choose a diary or journal, instead of social media or group texts, to record your feelings and personal thoughts. Many studies show that journaling can improve mental health, creativity, self-confidence, and mood. Do this daily as time allows.

PERSONAL STYLE CHOICES
Personalize your room to reflect what you love. Be creative, and don't feel like you have to make it look perfect like a magazine.

GAMES AND PUZZLES
Keep easy-to-pick-up activities like cards, Rubik's Cubes, crossword puzzles, knitting, etc., out in full view. What you have access to is what you will do. This will set you up for making good choices to fill downtime.

VISIBLE SPORTS EQUIPMENT
Experts say we make better choices when the good choice is in plain view. If you want to be more active, keep the necessary equipment out, like running shoes, to remind you to be active.

DOOR DECORATIONS
Decorate the front of your bedroom door. Changing it up for the seasons is a fun, creative way to make your room reflect your style and personality.

INSTRUMENTS
Keep an instrument in your room that you can easily pick up and learn to play—it is a relaxing way to fill downtime.

WALL CALENDAR
Staying organized with a wall calendar to write down activities is an important tip to start good habits. Keep it updated and put it by the door so you can check it when you walk out.

PLANT OR GOLDFISH
Keeping a plant or pet alive is a great way to practice responsibility and build good habits. Goldfish are easy to care for and relaxing to watch. Aquariums (even small goldfish bowls) can reduce anxiety and lower blood pressure.

NO MIRROR
No mirror in your bedroom? Yep! Take a break from being tempted to always look at yourself. Our culture spends way too much time focusing on appearance. Get out of that trap! A mirror in the bathroom is all you need.

MEMORY DISPLAY
Good memories, accomplishments, and things you love should be displayed to help you feel better and remember the fun days on the not-so-fun days.

GIVEAWAY BOX
Pull out the giveaway box every few months to purge things you no longer need, like outgrown sports equipment, books, clothes, and video games!

NO TV
Make your room a calm place. Leave no room for a TV or any other screen in your sanctuary.

BASKETBALL HOOP
An over-the-door hoop provides many benefits. It is perfect for working on coordination skills and brain development as it activates both sides of the brain. The added bonus is that it provides little healthy bursts of dopamine when you score.

ALARM CLOCK
Remember, you will need an alarm clock, not your mom or smartphone, to wake you up every morning. Get one with backup batteries in case the electricity goes out.

BOOKS AND MAGAZINES
Refresh your bookshelf so you have an assortment of interesting books that are easy to access.

ART SUPPLIES
You never know when the mood will strike to be creative, so keep your art supplies handy.

BOOK LIGHT
A book light attached to your headboard makes reading in bed really easy.

FAMILY PHOTO
Keep a family photo by your bed so it is the last thing you see before you go to sleep. Remembering that you belong to a family who loves you and has your back at the end of the day is good for your mental health!

DOWNTIME ROUTINES

Another big part of changing your environment is changing your downtime routines. If you're used to filling all your downtime by watching videos, scrolling through social media, or gaming, you will want to replace those habits with healthier activities that will make you feel better.

Consider discovering a cool new hobby or getting creative to make your downtime more exciting. Keep a list of fun and creative activities to avoid getting stuck in the screen trap—having a plan really helps. Make it easy for yourself by keeping these activities within reach and hiding those tempting screens. Your awesome and engaging alternatives are just a step away!

"Without screens constantly distracting me, I have the time to participate in all of the activities I love and try new ones. The more time I spend on screens, the more tired I feel and the less I want to participate in activities I once loved. With the decreased screen time, my mood improves, and I feel more excitement about everyday activities."

—Annalise, ScreenStrong Teen

ARE YOU AFRAID OF BEING BORED?

Sometimes, we are afraid of being bored. However, scientific research indicates that boredom is a good thing. We can tap into our innovation and creativity when we give our brains a break and allow our minds to wander without screens absorbing our attention.

Boredom makes us better, so don't shy away from being bored sometimes because being bored can do us so much good. Review the boredom busters on the next page and add some of your own ideas to the list.

"The free time I had because of my family's decision to be ScreenStrong allowed me to invest in dance, theater, speech and debate, baking, and music. I developed gifts for singing and public speaking, which have been invaluable to me as an adult."

—Aubrey, ScreenStrong college student

BOREDOM-BUSTERS!

Can you think of more ideas? Write them here!

SECTION 2
HOW DO I TRADE SCREEN TIME FOR MORE FUN?

"Why did the cats ask for a piano?
They wanted to make MEW-sic!"

Skippy, The ScreenStrong Cat

"My family decided to be ScreenStrong when I was in third grade. Everyone said I wouldn't have any friends but what happened is that I have a lot of friends! My brother and I plan a lot of fun get-togethers, and lots of people come. We used to plan a lot of sandlot baseball, shoot hoops in the driveway, plan get-togethers where we played our music, and I had a garage band in middle school. Even as a senior, I still didn't have a smartphone. But I was voted student body president that year. And I'm so thankful that I have good friends!"

—Evan, ScreenStrong Teen

REPLACE SCREENS WITH OTHER HOBBIES

You will need to find replacement activities to stop your screen habit—or any unwanted habit. Now is the time to try new hobbies. Join a club, work out, learn a new skill, take music lessons, get a job, write a kids' book for your little sister, or knit hats for the premature babies at your local hospital like Sarah, a ScreenStrong Teen, does. She says, *"I'm not on social media because I don't want to get addicted to it or waste time on it. I don't want to be obsessed with looking at other people's lives. I'm busy, and I'm doing a lot of other things, and I'm loving it!"*

The list of fun things to do and new hobbies to learn is endless! Here are a few ideas to jump-start your imagination.

FUN THINGS TO DO

HAVE MORE FUN WITH FAMILY

We need accountability to stop an unwanted habit or addiction. We are better off when we turn to our families and other caring grown-ups for support. Like a team that works together to help everyone succeed, family will unconditionally love and support us even if we are struggling.

When we're off our screens, we have a lot more time to strengthen our relationships with our families. Not only that, but it's so much nicer not to be arguing with our parents about our screen use all the time.

Here are some ideas for how we can have more fun with our family.

FAMILY FUN

DO MORE WITH FRIENDS

Here's some good news: when we're ScreenStrong, we will increase our chances of having deeper friendships. We don't have to be alone on our screens anymore. Having fun with friends in person is an excellent reward for breaking a screen habit. Everything is more fun when we share it with someone.

Think of a few friends who will try new hobbies with you.

FRIEND FUN

SECTION 3
WHAT IS MY NEW GAME PLAN?

"You don't have 9 lives.
Celebrate being ScreenStrong right MEOW!"
Skippy, The ScreenStrong Cat

When we begin our new ScreenStrong adventure, we will discover so much freedom in the ScreenStrong values listed below.

LIST ONE PERSONAL CHANGE YOU CAN MAKE UNDER EACH VALUE.

BUILD FAMILY CONNECTIONS

* ______________________
____

SAY NO TO TOXIC SCREENS

* ______________________
____

CHOOSE TO BE IN PERSON

* ______________________
____

PUT LIFE SKILLS FIRST

* ______________________
____

DARE TO BE DIFFERENT

* ______________________
____

THE SEVEN-DAY CHALLENGE

©screenstrong.org

GET YOUR FRIENDS OR YOUR WHOLE CLASS TO DO THE 7-DAY CHALLENGE

READY TO HAVE SOME FUN ?

Imagine an entire week of having fun with your friends without the constant stress of screens. Teens worldwide are taking the Challenge: putting down their phones and video games and discovering how freeing it can be. Here's what they are saying about taking the 7-Day Challenge with their class:

"More conversations at school were started to plan fun activities to fill our phone-free time over the weekend."

"I was able to spend the hour-long bus ride to my basketball game working on my vocabulary instead of mindlessly using my phone or scrolling through social media. I was more 'in the moment' with my family, and I had longer conversations with them."

"I not only got more sleep but I woke up later because I shockingly did not care as much about how I looked. I was not constantly looking at myself in the phone camera for the right picture to send to my friends. The freedom to not care about looking 'perfect' was relieving."

"I created more 'mental memories' than 'digital memories'—and those can never be deleted."

"I am a shy introvert who finds it difficult to strike up conversations with people I do not know. During the challenge, face-to-face conversation was my only means of communication. I began to talk to people I normally would never talk to."

"By the third day, I was actually happy to be off my phone, not having to worry about what people had sent me or how long I took to respond. It was nice that no one was on their phones because we were all doing the challenge."

THE 7-DAY CHALLENGE

Everyone takes a week off video games and social media and plans in-person get-togethers after school. It's tons of fun. Talk with your parents and teachers about how to make this happen, and have them **scan this QR code for more information about joining Connect.**

SCAN ME

THE 30-DAY CHALLENGE

Interested in a full detox? Check out our 30-Day Challenge, exclusively for our **Connect Plus** members.

7 CHALLENGE

screenSTRONG
7-DAY CHALLENGE

WHY THE 7-DAY CHALLENGE IS FOR YOU

→ You will have a **BREAK** from your parents constantly trying to get you off your screens! This means fewer arguments and conflicts. There will be more peace in your home.

→ You will experience less **STRESS** and anxiety related to social media. You won't have to "keep up" or "impress" anyone. You will have more time to relax.

→ You will **DISCOVER** that it will take you less time to do homework because you will not be distracted by your video games and smartphones. This will give you more free time to try new things.

→ You will have **TIME** to learn a new hobby or pick up an old one!

CHALLENGE RULES

Video Games / Tablets / iPads
Absolutely NO gaming devices, big or small. Box them up, and get them out of the house.

Child / Teen Smartphone
Time to hand over your phone to your parents, and they will make it disappear for seven days.

Social Media
No social media (Facebook, Instagram, Snapchat, TikTok, etc.)

School Screens
School screens are allowed for homework only.

TV
Keep the TV turned off, except for family movie nights.

PLAN AHEAD

TELLING TIME
Ask your parents for an alarm clock for your room and an inexpensive wristwatch. A clock for the bathroom is a good idea, too.

GATHER GOOD BOOKS
Do you have your own library card? Now is a great time to get one! Get some good books to read before you get started. You won't believe how much you will read when you aren't wasting time on your phone or video game. Ask your parents for a book light for your bed when reading at night. As an alternative, consider audiobooks.

OUTDOOR EQUIPMENT
Check the air in your bike tires and basketballs, and make sure you can find other things for outdoor activities: street hockey supplies, baseball equipment, a tire swing, and maybe a fire pit for the backyard.

ART SUPPLIES & JOURNALS
Gather your art supplies. Ask your parents for a journal. It's best to put private thoughts in a journal, not on social media! Write a basic schedule for the week. Write a simple weekly schedule of what you want to do this week.

PLAN A FRIDAY NIGHT SOCIAL
Friday night this week is designed for a planned social at your house with your friends. A board game night, fire pit and s'mores. Decide what you want to do now and start making your list of people to invite and what food you will need to get.

THE RESULTS

YOU WILL HAVE BETTER FRIENDSHIPS
Everyone wins when your friends hang out at your house instead of in the virtual world. All of you will be less lonely, you'll create great memories, and you'll be happier.

YOU WILL CREATE HEALTHY FAMILY CONNECTIONS
Choosing to connect with your family over peers may seem odd at first. Whether you rebuild that lost relationship or experience a brand-new connection, we all long for this connection. It's healthy and needed as you grow into a young adult.

YOU WILL EXPERIENCE FREEDOM FROM TOXIC SCREENS
Technology can be a useful tool, but toxic screen use—video games, social media, and pornography—is harmful and NOT mandatory for you. It is possible for you to be free from the stress and worry these screen activities cause.

YOU WILL GAIN NEW HOBBIES AND LIFE SKILLS
Replacing unnecessary screen time with real hobbies is so much fun. Imagine all the things you can learn. Start making a list. You are creative and smart; start exploring new things that will help you unfold into the amazing person you have been created to be.

YOU WILL EXPERIENCE LESS PAIN
When you learn to stand out from the crowd, chances are you will have less pain through your teen years. You will prevent the rejection pain from social media and possibly prevent a screen addiction down the road. Standing out from the crowd also makes it easier to be a leader!

START HERE
STEP 1: RECRUIT YOUR TRIBE
ASK FRIENDS TO DO MORE FUN, OFFLINE THINGS TOGETHER
ORGANIZE SOCIAL ACTIVITIES AFTER SCHOOL TOGETHER
PLAN YOUR FIRST FRIDAY FUN NIGHT AT YOUR HOUSE!
STEP 2: REPLACE SCREEN TIME WITH OTHER FUN THINGS
MAKE A LIST OF HOBBIES AND NON-SCREEN ACTIVITIES THAT INTEREST YOU
5. NATURE WALK
6. GO FISHING
7. GET A JOB
- PET SITTING
- MOW LAWN
8. WALK DOG
9. PLAY CARDS
17. RIDE BIKE
18. PLAY OUTSIDE
19. READ
EXCHANGE YOUR SMARTPHONE FOR A BASIC PHONE, AND VIDEO GAMES FOR BOARD GAMES
STEP 3: BE BOLD & BE SCREENSTRONG!
START THE 30 DAY SCREENSTRONG CHALLENGE
MONDAY
GO PLAY OUTSIDE!
meet friends at the park to ride bikes!
TUESDAY
FAMILY READING PARTY WITH POPCORN!
WEDNESDAY
HELP COOK DINNER (and dessert!) ← yum!
THURSDAY
PRACTICE MUSICAL INSTRUMENT
Ask mom about her favorite music when she was younger
FRIDAY
FRIDAY FUN NIGHT!
SAT.
FAMILY CONNECTION DAY!
SUN.
VISIT NATURE MUSEUM
CELEBRATE! YOU ARE NEARLY THERE!
CONGRATS! YOU MADE IT!

LET'S WRAP UP

Adam once told me, *"Mom, I regret all the time I spent playing video games; I don't have many fun childhood memories with my friends. Please tell my story to as many kids as possible so it won't happen to them. Tell them it is way easier to prevent screen problems than to recover from them."*

In this book, I have included everything my son Adam and our family wished we had known before we got caught in the screen addiction trap. You are so fortunate to have the facts now so you can be empowered to make the best choices. Here is the summary of your **two options**: one path can lead to anxiety and sadness, and the other leads to more adventures with friends and more happiness.

1ST PATH LEADS TO SCREEN ADDICTION & DEPENDENCY

2ND PATH LEADS TO FREEDOM: THE SCREENSTRONG LIFESTYLE

WHAT PATH WILL YOU CHOOSE?

I hope you and your parents choose the ScreenStrong way—a path you'll never regret. Childhood is a once-in-a-lifetime opportunity to **build real memories, discover passions, and create meaningful connections.** Screens will always be there, but this is your chance to experience life fully, freely, and without regrets.

Remember to stand out from the crowd & stay ScreenStrong!

Melanie

YOU WIN!
YOU ARE SCREENSTRONG!
CONGRATULATIONS!
©screenstrong.org

More Fish Less Screens
STAND OUT STAY STRONG
SAVE THE BRAINS
SCREENSTRONG
STAY STRONG
STAND OUT FROM THE CROWD
Bee ScreenStrong
DARE to be DIFFERENT

ABOUT THE AUTHOR

MELANIE HEMPE, BSN

When her oldest son was in middle school, Melanie Hempe noticed he was spending more and more time hunched over a screen, playing video games. Over time, these games became his whole world—he lost interest in sports, friends, and family. He was slipping into another reality, a virtual one. And eventually, he couldn't get out. You probably know kids like him. Or maybe that's you.

This was over a decade ago. Back then, like most parents, Melanie didn't realize how addictive video games and social media could be—until her son's gaming addiction caused the once A-student to drop out of college. Determined to help her family, Melanie, a nurse with a degree from Emory University, dove into research on how screens affect the brain. What she discovered stunned her. The harmful effects of excessive screen use on the developing brain are well-documented. By founding ScreenStrong, Melanie is now sharing this science with as many families as possible, helping them prevent and reverse screen addiction in their homes.

Melanie's bold, proactive approach—eliminating the most toxic screens (social media, video games, smartphones, and pornography) during the most impressionable stages of childhood—works. It fosters strong mental health, builds essential life skills, and strengthens friendships and family bonds.

Today, Melanie, her husband, and their four children live in North Carolina, where they're grateful to have traded screen overuse for real-life memories, strong relationships, and lasting fun. It's never too late to get your kids back and become a ScreenStrong family!

ACKNOWLEDGMENTS

A heartfelt thank you to Dr. Adriana Stacey, MD; Dr. Victoria Dunckley, MD; Dr. Leonard Sax, MD, PhD; Richard Freed, PhD; Douglas Gentile, PhD; Cris Rowan, OT; Dr. John Hutton, MD; Lt. Col. David Grossman; Tom Kersting; Joe Clement; and Matt Miles for their invaluable research and professional expertise.

We are also deeply grateful to our ScreenStrong Team—Mandee Hamann, Olivia Kernekin, Amie Robillard, Anna Wight, and Liz Breen—and the hundreds of ScreenStrong Ambassadors around the world for their dedication to our mission to prevent and reverse screen addiction. A special thanks to Lydia Hamann, Hallie Kate Oldham, Andrew and Evan Hempe, and our growing number of ScreenStrong students for their unique support and contributions to this important mission.

DESIGN

Artwork: Drobnick Designs, LLC
Cover Design: Drobnick Designs, LLC
Layout: Anna Wight

EDITORS

Amy Eytchison, Becky Grant, Anneka Daniell, Jennifer Ruisch, Josh Carlton, Dr. Adriana Stacey, MD, Olivia Kernekin, Andrew Hempe

KIDS' BRAINS & SCREENS
STUDENT EDITION

Empower your students to overcome screen addiction! This engaging, science-backed curriculum brings brain science to life, helping students see how screens impact their mental health, focus, relationships, and future success.

Designed to **spark curiosity, encourage critical thinking, and inspire real change**, it teaches the "why" behind addiction science. This course will motivate students to think critically, set emotions aside, and make smarter screen choices—building healthier screen habits that will **last a lifetime**.

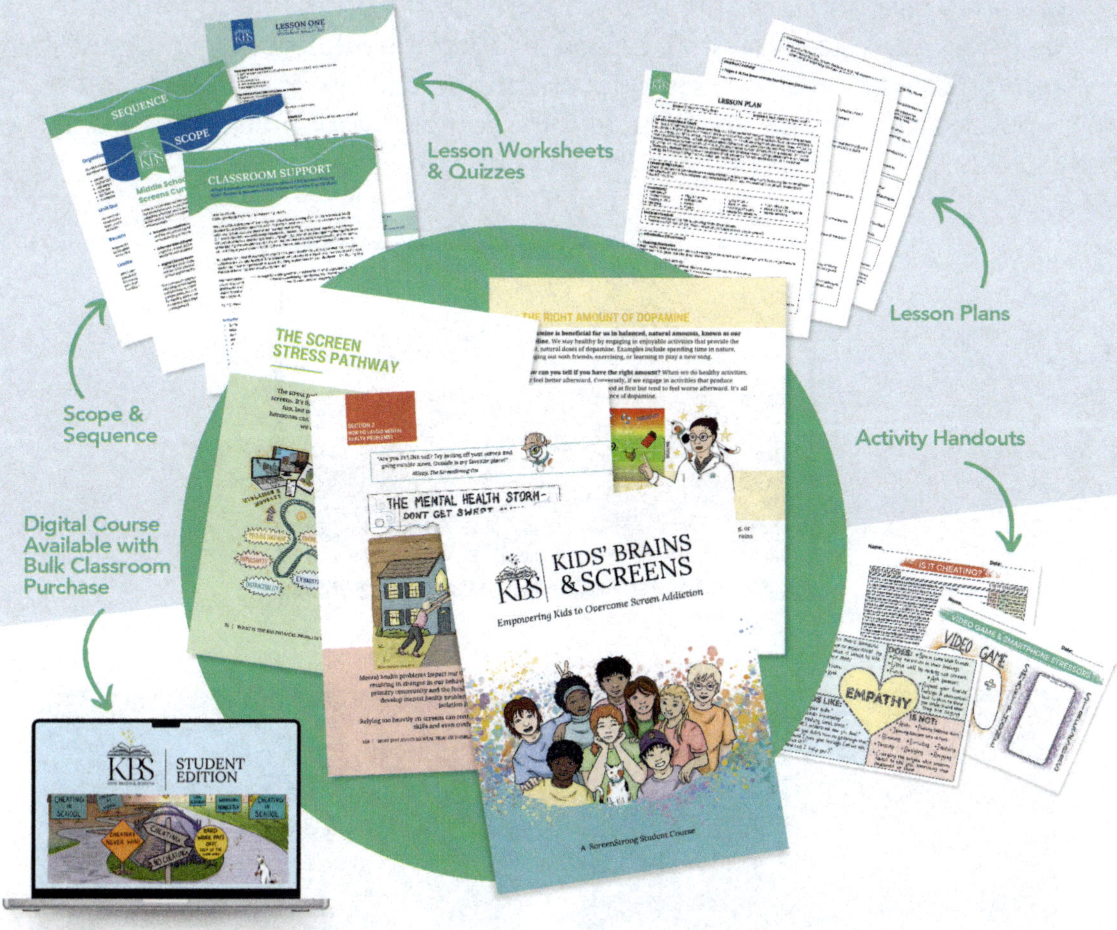

- ✓ Eight Colorful Lessons *(three sections each)*
- ✓ Lesson Worksheets and Quizzes
- ✓ 24 Lesson Plans
- ✓ Scope and Sequence
- ✓ Activity Handouts
- ✓ Video Content
- ✓ 7-Day Challenge Screen Detox for Classrooms
- ✓ 200+ Ways to Unplug
- ✓ Friday Fun Night Instructions
- ✓ Escape from Screen Jail Bonus Challenge
- ✓ Q&A
- ✓ Digital Course Access with Bulk Classroom Purchase

To learn more about the school curriculum go to: kidsbrainsandscreens.com

KIDS' BRAINS & SCREENS
THE ADVENTURES OF SUPER BRAIN

Help Your Child Trade Screen Time for Real-Life Adventures

The Adventures of Super Brain is a fun, science-based story that helps 3rd- and 4th-grade students understand how their amazing brains grow—and how excessive screen time can hold them back.

Packed with colorful illustrations, playful characters, and powerful brain facts, ***The Adventures of Super Brain*** helps families spark the right conversations at just the right time—before screen habits become screen struggles. Kids will love meeting their Super Brain, defeating the sneaky villain MegaDrain, and discovering why real-life adventures—not screen time—are what their amazing brains need to grow strong. Perfect for classrooms, family reading, and school libraries.

- Makes brain science fun and engaging
- Includes four easy-to-read chapters
- Explains screen addiction science in easy terms
- Includes discussion questions for home or classroom use

To learn more about Super Brain visit: kidsbrainsandscreens.com

IT'S TIME TO TELL YOUR SCHOOL!

Phone-Free Schools

Using brain science education to inform and support an effective phone-free policy

A Guide For School Administrators
Provided by ScreenStrong

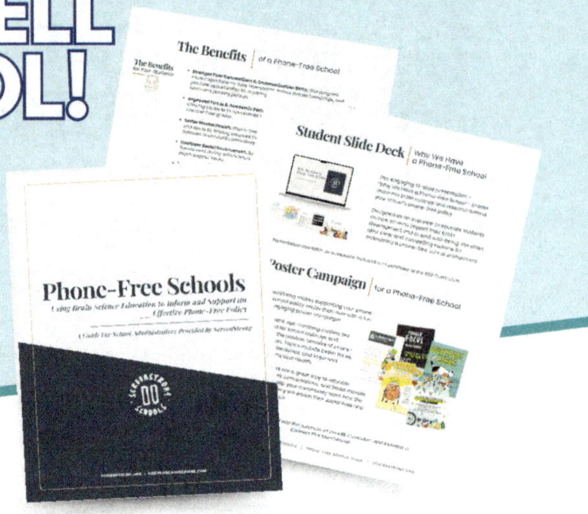

What You Get In Our FREE Guide:

- The stats & benefits of a phone-free school
- A complete sample phone-free policy
- Tips for educating your students and parent community
- Letter to teachers & parents
- Sample FAQs
- Ideas for recruiting volunteers to be Phone-Free school Champions

---

Bonus Material:

- School Assembly Slides & Talking Points
- School SCREEN Awareness Poster Series for Elementary, Middle and High School

To learn more about the ScreenStrong Schools: screenstrong.org/schools

Printed in Dunstable, United Kingdom

63753134R00138